Re-Branding Yourself after Age 50

Recharge your Career, Start a Business or Achieve More Professional Success in Midlife

By

MARVA L. GOLDSMITH, AICI CIP

CONTRIBUTING EDITORS
Alicia M. Nails
Max Gordon

FEATURED AUTHORS
Art Lizza
Carla Dancy Smith
Dean Moss
Satori Shakoor
Sue Thompson
Deborah Porter

CONTRIBUTING AUTHORS
Albert Edwards III, PhD
Ann Middleman
Edith Wagner
Jim Sniechowski, PhD
Judith Sherven, PhD
Michael Levy
Dr. Nancy Irwin
Pamela Faulkner
Ron Tannebaum
Steve Letsinger
Sue Ellen Endicott
Wray Rives

ILLUSTRATOR
George Blesson

Branding Yourself after Age 50
First Publication: March 2009
Second Publication: September 2009

Re-Branding Yourself After Age 50
Third Publication: September 2010

Copyright @ 2009
Marva Goldsmith & Associates, Inc.
All rights reserved.

No part of this book may be used or reproduced in any manner without written permission except in the case of brief quotations.
ISBN: 1-4537544-5-8

Acknowledgments

This book is dedicated to my mother. She is my hero. At the age of 51, after more than three decades spent working in the Detroit Police Department (DPD), my mother's determination and financial acumen enabled her to take the brave step of "early out."

She started working for the DPD after high school at the age of 18 and continued working after marrying my father and giving birth to my sister Marcia followed by me two years later. After their divorce, she raised us, instilling the same determination and pride of accomplishment that led us both to become successful engineers in the 1980s – a time when female minorities were far from common.

Once Marcia and I were married, my mother opted for early retirement and moved to Tacoma, Washington, with her twin sister, who retired from Detroit Receiving Hospital. At the time of this writing, they are 77 years old. They have spent the past 25 years, a full third of their lives, living well without having to work another day in what has truly been their "Golden Age."

I began writing this book in the summer of 2008 while on my way to Little Rock, Arkansas, to attend my family reunion. With my December 5th birthday looming, the idea of turning 50 was often in my thoughts. While preparing for the inevitable reunion question, "What are you up to these days?" I pondered this looming milestone.

This book started as a reflection piece…therapy – yes, self-imposed therapy – and turned into something much more than I had imagined or planned. I am truly grateful to everyone who contributed to this book, including those whose stories you will read and others who were behind the scenes editing, reading early drafts, or just cheering me on.

Special thanks go to Satori Shakoor, Sue Thompson, Art Lizza, Mike Levy, Ann Middleman, Judith Sherven, PhD, Jim Sniechowski, PhD, Dr. Nancy Irwin, Wray Rives, Dean Moss, Pamela Faulkner, Dr. Albert Edwards, III, Deborah Porter, Ron Tannebaum, Steve Letsinger, Christy Zorn, Carla Dancy Smith, Alicia Nails, Max Gordon, Lisa Merriam, Deborah Porter, Edith Wagner, Sue Ellen Endicott, Kathleen Tracy, Paul Watkins, Sage Evans and Christa Davison for their contributions to the book. Thanks are also due to Walter O'Bryant, Vanessa Weathersby, Mary Artz, and Frank Mitchell for their review and comments.

I am especially grateful for my family and friends who helped me usher in my second half-century of blissful living on a wintry evening in Detroit: Sheryl Shanklin, Preston Shanklin, Bernadine Miller, Andre DuPerry, Crystal Roberts, Michael Wagner, Tim and Rose Lucas, James Moore, Leland and Joyce Stein, George and Linda Stein, Vanessa Weathersby, Wesley Sewood, Sheila Spencer, Janna and Satchel Garrison, Alicia Nails, Venesta Jones, Tommy Stallworth, Nicole Wells, and especially my loving sister, Marcia Jackson, who made my celebration possible.

I'd also like to extend my gratitude to the pioneers of personal branding: Tom Peters, credited with coining the phrase and starting the revolution, William Arruda, an innovator and creative genius and Peter Montoya, whose book *The Brand Called You* led me to the exploration.

I hope this book will inspire some direction or purpose or simply encourage you to live out your bliss…and to be your own "best brand."

Happy 50th!

Contents

INTRODUCTION	1
CHAPTER ONE: What's Age Got to Do with It?	9
Turning 50 is different than turning 30 or 40	10
Nobody warned me about turning 50	11
CHAPTER TWO: Problem…or Opportunity?	13
A classic parable	13
The Iceberg Exercise	19
CHAPTER THREE: The Pursuit of Happiness	27
My Own "Then"	28
Art's Story	28
Art's SWOT	36
In My Experience: Steve Letsinger	38
CHAPTER FOUR: So, What Do You Want?	41
Your SWOT	47
STRENGTHS	47
Unique selling proposition: Your sweet spot	50
In My Experience: Michael Levy	50
In My Experience: Sue Ellen Addicott	56
CHAPTER FIVE: Branding: What It Is…and What It Ain't	63
Ketchup	63
What is personal branding?	64
Dennis Rodman: A Unique Personal Brand	70
In My Experience: Judith Sherven, PhD and Jim Sniechowski, PhD	72
In My Experience: Edith Wagner	82

CHAPTER SIX: Applying Branding Principles to Your Product – You!	89
Leadership	89
Visibility	90
Consistency	90
Brand Strategy review	92
Art re-visited	92
Art's Brand Strategy	93
CHAPTER SEVEN: Passion and Branding	99
In My Experience: Ron Tannebaum	100
CHAPTER EIGHT: Sue's Story	107
Sue's personal inventory	113
Sue's goal	113
Sue's SWOT	114
A conversation between Sue and Marva	115
In My Experience: Pamela Faulkner	117
CHAPTER NINE: The Retreat	121
Keys to good health and well-being	123
Peer review	129
CHAPTER TEN: Lessons from Dolly: Your Package	133
Tips for the 50+ job seeker	135
Speaking style	137
Body language	137
CHAPTER ELEVEN: Vision – A Gift…and a Curse	143
Exploring your vision: It's a gift and a curse	144
Marva's vision for NOW	146
CHAPTER TWELVE: You Can't Get from THEN to NOW without ACTION	149
October 13, 2008	149
My pet rock – make that e-rock!	150
In My Experience: Dr. Albert Edwards, III	151

CHAPTER THIRTEEN: Social Media Revolution 153
So, what is "Web 2.0" social media? 156
Why is social media so effective? 157
What about Twitter? 158
Karen's tips to Twitter success 159
Deborah's Story 160

CHAPTER FOURTEEN: Ready, Camera, ACTION! 163
Power-filled actions! 163
Art's One-Week Power Plan 164
In My Experience: Wray Rives 170

What I Did For Love: The Quest of a Lifelong Learner 173

Fifty and Fabulous, Darling…Choosing and Meeting the
Challenge of a Lifetime 178

Dance Like Nobody's Watching 185

Conclusion…But Not the End 189

Appendix:
Survey Questions 191
The Authors 203

INTRODUCTION

A flight of fancy at 50

July 24

I hear and feel the familiar thud of the plane's doors closing tightly and then the plane shudders into motion. We roll toward the runway and I begin to say a little prayer as we prepare for takeoff. Halfway through the prayer, it hits me! I open one eye in excitement but decide to finish the prayer – always a good idea before takeoff – then I return to my inspiration.

Finally, after months of agonizing thought, I know what I want to do for my birthday. It's not just any birthday. On December 5th, I will turn 50.

The pressure to do something in celebration of that all-important 50th birthday is enormous. Well, at least it has been for me. Think about it: the half-century mark!

"How old are you?" I imagine being asked.

"Half a century," I will say.

Shall I have a party? Should I have it in Detroit, where I've lived most of my life…or in Maryland, where I currently reside? Decisions, decisions. The pressure!

Perhaps I'll just take the "no worries" solution and live vicariously through my sister – retroactively. She had a fabulous 50th celebration two years earlier. Her last guest didn't leave until four o'clock the next morning. I had a blast! We danced, laughed, drank, ate, then we danced some more. As a matter of fact, I seem to have many friends and family members turning 50 these days. Perhaps instead of hosting one big party, I will celebrate my birthday at every other 50th celebration I attend.

I thought about going to a mind and body cleansing retreat; some type of health farm, rejuvenation spa, or women's retreat. I researched Sedona, the Crossings in Austin, and Life Launch in Santa Barbara, where I could indulge in healthy exercise and food, as well as yoga, meditation, daily massage, sitar music, bean sprouts – you know, the whole transcendental experience. Rise with the sun and reflect on life. Just take a "time out." Leave the Black*(crack)*Berry® and the laptop at home and take time to just BE. I'm still thinking about this idea; it sounds pretty refreshing.

I also thought about taking a cruise in the Caribbean with someone special; or going island-hopping with a group of friends for fun, shopping, cosmos, and just mixing it up – somewhat the opposite end of the spectrum from the cleansing retreat idea. I haven't ruled out those options.

Since it will take me another five months to write this book, you may find out that I did the spa trip or took a cruise after all. (In fact, I know I would enjoy finishing up the final writing of this book on a beach in St. Lucia, Puerto Rico, or St. Martin!)

But what was it, you may be wondering, that "hit me" as my flight was taking off?

You're holding it right now.

I thought, *I'll write a book on turning 50!*

An old idea with a new direction

Okay, it's not a new idea. Many people have written books about turning 50. Many of the books are celebrity autobiographies; the personal lives and careers, up to and including the 50-year milestone, of the famous and infamous.

This book will be different. This book isn't by or for people who think that their best years lie behind them, or those who long for the glory and smooth skin of their salad days. No, *this* book will focus on the rest of us and will be a guide to recharging your personal brand *after* age 50. It is intended to jumpstart, re-fuel, or re-charge your passions and interest – especially for those in need of a little boost. It will *not* be about nostalgia or the search for the Fountain of Youth but about the rest – and the best – that is yet to come. New beginnings. Renewal. Reinvention.

Reinvention is the new "Buzzword"

Baby Boomers everywhere are in the process of reinventing themselves. According to *American Demographics Magazine*, seven baby boomers will turn 50 every minute in the United States from now until 2014, and there are more than 16 million Americans over age 55 that are either working or seeking work. If you need to kick it into gear *after* the **Big 5-0**, you'll get plenty of inspiration and information from this book.

In 2004, the Queen of Reinvention, Madonna, named her tour the "Re-Invention Tour." But what can we 50-year-olds learn from Madonna (whose 50th birthday preceded mine by five months)?

- She uses innovation to manage her career.
- Constant reinvention enables her to remain relevant to ever-changing needs and desires of the marketplace.
- She manages her brand with great intentionality.

What is personal branding?

What is personal branding and why do you need to think about it? According to Peter Montoya, a personal brand is "an identity that stimulates precise, meaningful perceptions in its audience about the values and qualities the person stands for." These perceptions vary as you move from one "domain" to another: home, business, community, and/or school. Your brand in your "business" domain is not going to be the same as your brand in your "home" domain: that is, your kids, significant other, or parents will not describe you using the same words as your business colleagues.

Personal branding is all about differentiating yourself from your competitors – the rest of the market. To do that, you need to understand what makes *you* unique and compelling. Ultimately, branding involves three important components: personality, position, and promise.

- **PERSONALITY** – A successful brand is packaged in such a way that you distinguish yourself from others while supporting the vision you have for your future. This does not mean you have to dress or behave in some outré fashion; only that YOU need to highlight your best features to be easily recognizable. Your packaging is an advertisement of the product. So be careful to send the right message at all times.

- **POSITION** – A successful brand provides added to value in order to determine its relative position amongst other products. The most successful brands can be described in a single sentence or phrase. "Like a rock" suggests that Chevy trucks are tough. "We'll leave the light on for you" says you're always welcome at Motel 6. What about YOU? Maybe "Pat Smith always gets things done," or "Terry Jones knows everything about sailing." If you are incredibly successful, sometimes your brand can be described by a single word as were Kleenex® and Xerox®. Think: Oprah, Madonna, Gandhi.

- **PROMISE** – A successful brand promises a particular experience. Online auctioneer eBay says "Buy it. Sell it. Love it." The whole experience is suggested by those six words: customers will find it easy to buy and sell, and they will be pleased with the results. What promise do YOU offer? Maybe you're a top-notch CPA who offers "worry-free tax preparation" or a coach for runners who wants to "train without pain."

Read the following excerpt from *The 22 Immutable Laws of Branding* (2002), by Al and Laura Ries. I've substituted the word "YOU" where it applies:

"...Branding in the marketplace is very similar to branding on the ranch. A branding program should be designed to differentiate YOU from all the 'cattle on the range.' Even if all the other cattle on the range look pretty much alike, the objective is to create in the mind of the prospect the perception that there is no other product on the market quite like YOU."

A new direction

I started my branding and personal development company, Marva Goldsmith & Associates (MG&A), in September 2001, thinking that starting the company was just something I would do while waiting for a C-level position (or at least a VP spot) to materialize. I had read an article that stated for every $100,000 in salary you seek, you needed to allow 12 to 18 months for your job search. So, I started MG&A as a placeholder, something to list on my resume as an "in the meantime" activity.

After a few months of self-employment, my fear of ending up as a bag lady was all but gone, surpassed by the joy I felt while helping others reshape their personal and professional images. Soon, I stopped looking for that C-level job altogether and started reinventing the brand known as Marva Goldsmith. This book offers a glimpse into the process I used to reinvent myself (*before* age 50) as well as an idea of how you can apply it to your own lives – at any age.

Supporting characters

Since I began writing this before I was 50, I could not legitimately offer the full experience of branding myself after age 50 so I invited a few other people to contribute to this book.

- **Art Lizza** is the primary case study we'll follow. "Downsized" *after* age 50, Art found his passion as a writer and is now working to reinvent himself as a full-time author.
- **Sue Thompson** started a motivation and public speaking business and lost 75 pounds – and she did it all **after** turning 50.
- **Satori Shakoor** celebrated her 50th birthday in fine form – by successfully competing in a bodybuilding competition.
- **Carla Dancy Smith** began her master's degree program at American University at the age of 50.
- Fifty-year-old **Deborah Porter** used social media to find a job in her field of expertise after six months of unemployment.
- **Dean Moss'** career in professional dance and choreography has soared in midlife.

If you are over 50, or approaching the "Golden Age," you have been developing a set of transferable skills for 20 or 30 years. Most likely these skills are still needed somewhere, even if it's not with your current or former employer. You are already a consultant with a brand of your own.

Over the past seven years, I have completely rewritten my professional script and roles: I've transitioned from being an engineer, federal lobbyist, and mid-level utility executive to being an image consultant, brand coach, national speaker, trainer, and entrepreneur. My resume is *not* defined by my past experience in corporate America.

Instead, it focuses on my desire for the next 15 years: to be a nationally recognized, highly sought-after, *well-paid* speaker and consultant who creates experiences that transform corporations, organizations, and individuals.

This book has been written using my experiences with personal and professional transformation, also known as reinvention. Many of you reading this book will find yourselves asking the same questions I asked myself in the face of change and surprises, especially the big question: *Is this a crisis…or an opportunity in disguise?* It all depends on your perspective. Here, the focus will be on you and your personal brand. What should you do now that the employment game has changed? If you fully engage, complete the exercises in this book, and *get into action*, a year from now you may look back and say, **Job uncertainty was the best thing that ever happened to me.**

To make this happen, this book will help you address three questions:

1. What do I want?
2. How do I get from "then" to "now"?
3. If not now, when?

Present…tense?

First, let's assess the present. Even at the age of 50, some of us have not fully explored the first question. Perhaps you've never taken the time to *ask* the question at all. It's easy to get caught up in everyday living, unconscious living – cruise control. I don't know about you, but I feel as if I just looked up one day and there it was – I was almost 50. It snuck up without warning. It's easy to understand how busy lives can detract from our ability to take time out and answer this important question of what we *really* want.

Throughout this book, you will find stories written by those who are living in their own "Golden Age;" people who know just what they want and are currently in hot pursuit of it. You will also read the stories of individuals who face branding challenges that relate to turning 50.

Although the focus of this book is on your professional life, it can also change your personal life as this book can be used as a vehicle to explore the pathways of your hopes and dreams to discover your **life's purpose**.

The "Golden Age" begins at 50

Before we proceed, let me define the term "Golden Age." For some, the term will conjure up images of the *Golden Girls* sitcom – cute and funny, but *old*.

GOLD is such a precious metal. It's been used almost since the dawn of human history to display wealth and importance and it has inherent qualities as well. Being relatively soft and malleable, it is an efficient conductor of both heat and electricity. Gold is resistant to the effects of moisture, oxygen, and corrosive elements.

People who have lived to their 50th year are like gold. We have certainly encountered a few corrosive elements, have had to be malleable and flexible, and have experienced many electric moments. We are precious metals. Indeed, at the Golden Age, we *should be* "highly sought-after" precious metals.

On the following pages, we'll explore the **Golden Age** together. What's in store for us? How can we best approach this wonderful time in our lives? What do we want? How are we *being* at 50?

As I reflect on this "turning 50" project, I hope this book has a broader reach, a wider appeal, and a more profound impact than a 50th birthday celebration. I hope it exhilarates others as much as any party, spa retreat, or lavish trip to an exotic destination, and brings a spark of renewal and rejuvenation to me *and* to you.

Consider this book to be an invitation to my birthday celebration. My birthday wish for you is that you will **commit to reinvention** and begin the work of recharging your personal brand after age 50. Some of you will find your transformation to be a reinvention. That's a positive form of change. Don't waste a moment!

The time to begin is **now**! Carpe diem!

CHAPTER ONE

What's Age Got to Do with It?

Copyright, Marva Goldsmith & Associates, Inc

As of this writing, I am single…and looking. Hello?!

I went on a date a few months ago with a man I met on a popular Internet dating site. My date worked in the entertainment industry. After a couple of hours we exchanged Internet dating horror stories – now that's always fun to do! We talked about how, during your first face-to-face meeting, it quickly becomes obvious (sometimes painfully so) if your date has an exaggerated sense of self; has used someone else's pictures for their profile; has led a really hard life since registering with the site; or is a master at reinventing the truth.

My eyes became as big as saucers when my date confessed that he did not tell the truth about two items in his online dating profile. *Please don't tell me you're married!* I can't remember the first trivial fib he confessed to, but the second was about his age. He had listed himself as 48 years old, when, in fact, he had just turned 50. He explained that entertainment is a very competitive industry and he was sensitive to the stigma of being an "old man" in a "young person's" industry, where people are routinely shuffled in and out of jobs based on others' perceptions that veterans may not be "fresh." I was reminded of a lyric from Harry Chapin's hit *WOLD*: "They said that they liked the younger sound when they let me go."

For some, the idea of turning 50 is daunting. For others, it's a new adventure. Clearly, my date had an issue with perception. Later, I considered his situation and thought he needed to ask himself some tough questions. How could he manage the way others perceive him? How could he prepare himself for what he believes to be the inevitable and untimely demise of his career? How could he effectively brand himself as a valuable, contributing player in a youth-focused industry even after the age of 50? *What can he learn from the reinvention role model, Madonna?*

Turning 50 is different than turning 30 or 40

When I turned 30 I felt like a grownup; as though I had suddenly blossomed into adulthood. Thirty had a very mature ring to it. For most, your 30s are the time you become the principal star of your own mini-series: your career is progressing and you have (consciously or not) established your personal "brand" in your work and community lives. People expect a certain level and range of experience from you based on what you usually deliver.

You are making money. You are making significant life choices during this decade. Professionally and personally, the opportunities before you seem limitless. Most significantly, you feel as though you have plenty of time left to choose among them.

Your sense of immortality begins to fade somewhat by your 40s and you aggressively pursue professional and personal goals. For many, that means nurturing and raising little people, too. At 40, you are in the headlong rush of real life. You are in the big leagues, playing the grownup game with skill, purpose, and a great deal of self-assurance and confidence. After all, you have accumulated a fair amount of experience. Your decisions affect others tremendously, both at home and at work, so you direct your focus on choosing wisely and making sound decisions. You are still young enough to play, but old enough to take full responsibility for your actions. Perhaps most important of all: You are responsible and accountable.

I think of turning 40 with glee – yes, absolute glee. I was a triple threat! My body, brain, and bank account were simultaneously in full throttle. In retrospect, I was fearless. *What the heck?* I thought. I was divorced, didn't have any children – what better time would there be to make some changes, take some risks, reinvent myself? I made a bold, life-altering decision to go back to school full-time, took a year off from the corporate world, and went to Harvard. Fun! Exciting! Geez, me at Harvard! I met people from all over the world. I had given myself a gift that significantly changed the trajectory of my life.

Nobody warned me about turning 50

I read in *O Magazine* (Oprah approved it, so it must be true) that every day 6,000 American women turn 50 years old. So I know there is a huge "amen corner" backing up my claim that turning 50 feels different from any other decade changeover. Physically, and perhaps emotionally, something is clearly different about 50. First, there's my physical inventory. I am certainly entering my 50s with a different physicality. Some of the changes are inevitable and apparently permanent. It appears that the laws of elasticity and gravity have serious implications for skin, tendons, and muscles as well. You can only stretch or stitch some of these body parts so far before they refuse to spring back or stay put.

I have accepted my own physical changes, like weight gain and hair loss. I have begun to do what I can to slow my body's natural aging process, eating "goo-gobs" of antioxidants, and joining both Weight Watchers and Curves. In fact, I've been told that I don't look 50 at all. (Thank you, Mom, for good genes.)

Inevitably, there is the post-50 professional inventory and some comparisons between what we had hoped to achieve and what we have actually accomplished or become. Some of our career choices may seem permanent. But must they be? Some opportunities may have passed us by but have they really been "lost" to us?

What about new opportunities and choices? Are they still limitless? Is it still possible to be a fearless and confident star going into our sixth decade?

I have used words like *star, fearless*, and *confidence* to describe the onset of my 30s and 40s, but my focus here will be what will mark this decade of the 50s – for me and for you. For these years we need a new set of words: *courageous, relentless, strong, happy, peaceful, graceful, exuberant, wise, spiritual, intuitive,* and *blessed* come to mind.

> ### EXERCISE
> It is important to have a place to record your thoughts as you read. I rarely read a book without a pen in my hand. As you go through this book, certain stories, ideas, and questions will resonate with you. Get in the habit of writing those precious thoughts down. For an example, answer the following question:
>
> What are you thinking? (Don't say, "Nothing." That's absolutely impossible because the mind never stops working.)

CHAPTER TWO

Problem...or Opportunity?

A classic parable

I do not recall when or from whom I first heard this, but the message is one for the ages.

> A farmer's donkey fell into an abandoned well. The donkey cried for hours while the farmer pondered what to do. Finally, he decided that since the donkey had lived a long life, and the well had to be filled in anyway, he would simply say a few words and bury the donkey in the well. He asked his neighbors to help him and everyone began shoveling dirt into the well. At first, the donkey cried even louder. Then, to everyone's amazement, he became quiet. Curious, the farmer looked into the well and was astonished to see that with each shovel of dirt that hit his back, the donkey would simply shake it off and step up onto

it. It was not long before the donkey was able to step over the edge of the well and trot happily away.

MORAL: Shake it off and step up!

Uncertain times, surprising opportunities

Crisis…depression…recession…or even just plain hard times – whatever you call the current international financial situation, the impact is the same: We are faced with a very uncertain employment and economic future.

Every decade brings some form of economic turmoil. In the 1970s, the U.S. economy saw high energy prices, high inflation, and high interest rates. The front-page headlines grew shrill with warnings of yet more layoffs and company closings. (Sound familiar?) During the 80s and 90s, the words "restructuring" and "downsizing" became staples in our business vocabulary. And now, a decade into the 21st century, we are seeing numerous industries shutting down, jobs moving overseas, and a demand for new skills. Even the "Big Three" U.S. automakers and "Big Blue" are no longer **big**. Marvin Gaye sang, "There are only three things for sure – taxes, death, and trouble."

I would modify the list to include *change*.

Change is an unstoppable force. Benjamin Disraeli, a 19th-century British writer and statesman, said, "Change is inevitable. Change is constant." For example, even in the best of times you could still lose your job or source of income. It doesn't matter whether you lose your job in a mass layoff, during a time of economic turmoil, or when everything is booming for everyone else. The moment you lose your job you are at a crossroad.

John F. Kennedy once observed, "When written in Chinese, the word 'crisis' is composed of two characters. One represents danger, and the other represents opportunity." So the question you must ask yourself is, "Will I treat this circumstance as a crisis or as an opportunity?"

I have learned to create "opportunity" from almost any set of circumstances – whether self-imposed or unplanned. After 20 years I chose to leave my comfortable corporate position at a major utility company and pursue my dreams. Seven years later I found myself surrounded by comrades in their 50s who were in the midst of "unplanned career outages."

Many people who face unemployment for the first time after 20 or 25 years of continuous employment are justifiably frightened after having been busily engaged in their careers. Some are high-flyers who have done nothing wrong – indeed, some were the driving forces behind the success of their respective companies yet nevertheless found themselves in the position of having to begin over again.

Remember the parable? Deep in a well, the donkey that was facing a crisis hesitated at first but soon recognized the dirt as an opportunity. Here's the deal: nothing is going to change the fact that you've lost your job, or promotion, or the funds you've invested. You cannot wish that job, promotion, pension, or golden parachute back into existence. Once the genie is out of the bottle, *it's not going back inside*. So now what? Learn to recognize that what's being shoveled onto your head may be the key to stepping up and out.

The Free Agent Nation

In 2001, I interviewed with Burson-Marsteller when I first arrived in Washington and was looking for a job. In retrospect, the interview was a colossal flop. I did not know what I wanted, nor could I articulate the value I could provide the PR giant. The colleague who secured the interview for me gave me a copy of Daniel Pink's Free Agent Nation. It was a tremendous gift! In the months to come, I read the book cover to cover and began to understand the new world of work. More importantly, I began to think differently about how I would approach my work.

When Pink wrote the book in 1997, he defined the residents of Free Agent, USA as 14 million self-employed Americans; 8.3 million independent contractors and 2.3 million people who find work each day through temporary agencies. Free Agents move from project to project, define their work and generally work on their own. The economic downturn of 2007 has turned many unexpecting employees into free agents. So, how can we embrace this new status and develop this new way of defining ourselves into a successful job search, new business or consultancy?

> "The Organization Man is history. Taking his place is America's new economic icon: the "Free agent" – the job-hopping, tech-savvy, fulfillment –seeking, self-reliant, independent worker. Already 30 million strong, these new "dis-organization" men and women are transform-

ing America in ways both profound and exhilarating." Daniel H. Pink, Author, Free Agent Nation, 1997

The stories that follow are of Baby Boomers who have embraced the concept of free agency:

- Free agents are introspective: you know (or explore) who you are and what you want to do with your life.
- Free agents seek work that is personal and meaningful: there is synchronicity between purpose and work.
- Free agents take responsibility: you provide all that is necessary for a first round draft pick to maintain a competitive edge (i.e., healthcare, training and development, technology enhancements).
- Free agents do not recognize borders: with Internet access, your work is global.
- Free agent work *should* be fun: if you are doing what you love, the work becomes an extension of you.

In My Experience...

It was June 2001. I was the Vice President of Research at a Public Relations firm. The economy had tanked, several clients had left the agency (some, without paying), and the agency cut 20 percent. Then, three months later, there was another round of layoffs. Even when "it's not personal, just business," it's always personal for the one being laid off. On the other hand, I was beginning to plan my exit from the firm because it had become a most unpleasant place in which to work. So part of me was relieved because I would receive severance pay and unemployment while I looked for a new job fulltime, rather than sneaking around on interviews.

I let everyone know I was looking. You never know when or where an opportunity will arise. I got my résumé in shape and then I went on Monster.com and posted it. I also began networking by attending professional meetings as often as possible.

New Business Start

The business came a few months later. But I used the same basic strategies: told everyone I knew that I'd started the new business and went to as many networking meetings as I could stand.

About a year into my business I hired a firm to put up my first web site. I made the investment because I wanted it done right and it is a representation of me. Two years later I hired a graphic artist (a friend from a networking group) to design a logo and then I hired another web designer to re-design my web site. I've stuck with that one: www.admmarketing.com.

Visibility: Getting the Word Out

I publish a monthly newsletter which I send to (pretty much) anyone I meet or know. This includes clients, former colleagues, networking friends, and people I meet at various meetings. The newsletter is my primary way of keeping in touch.

Another important source of referrals has been an industry directory. Listing my company in the directory has resulted in several major projects so I expand it each year. It's a great investment – a very good ROI.

What lessons or insights would you share with others in a similar position? First off, don't feel too depressed if you are downsized or laid off. It happens to a lot of people, even those who have worked for their employers for a very long time. It's usually not personal so just put one foot in front of the other and start over.

Even before you've recovered from the shock, begin to network. Don't be afraid to tell people you've been downsized (it's certainly better than saying you've been fired!). Then network some more. Find new sources for networking: have lunch with former colleagues, go to professional meetings.

If you want to switch gears, you must decide what you want to do. Is it a different segment of the industry you are already in? Do you want to consult with people or firms about the kind of work you had been doing?

If it's a different industry then you have some homework to do. If you know someone, or you are referred to someone in that industry, pick their brains. Find out where the opportunities are. Find out what you should be charging. Find out who gives out the work (referral sources).

If you want to go into an e-tailing business or manufacturing, then you have even more homework to do. You may have to take a course to learn about process, regulations, licensing, and more. But learn what is necessary before you charge into it.

And then network, network, network. Use social media, by all means. You may need to take a class to learn about that, too. Nearly every professional group has had programs about social media. Find out who is offering those programs and go. Go to them all. You'll learn something a little different at each one.

What advice would you give or did you receive that was most helpful throughout the changes you made?

When I was first laid off, a former client referred me to a business writer who lived near me. I called her and she invited me to a meeting of the IABC. That meeting changed my life because I met a man there who worked for an ad agency that did a lot of branding work. Two weeks later he asked me to come to a client meeting with him and we sold the project that launched my business.

So the bottom line is: let everyone know what you are doing. Seek information and advice from trusted friends, colleagues, and clients. Look for opportunities but don't charge headlong into something new without knowing where the obstacles and speed bumps are.

Is there anything else that you want to share with others...words of wisdom?

Being an entrepreneur is not for everyone. First, you have to *run* your business as well as *do* the work – unless you have a partner and that can be tricky, too. Second, understand your strengths and weaknesses: Don't try to be someone you aren't. If you are not a good writer, for example, take a course or buy a book or hire a writer. If you are not a good salesperson, or you feel especially uncomfortable selling, do the same thing: take a course, get a partner, or hire a sales rep.

And if entrepreneurship is not for you, I'd still advise outreach and networking to find a job. Yes, you can go on Ladders or Monster, or a more traditional approach. But the fact is that most jobs are filled through personal recommendations, so work it! Use social media to make connections and maintain them. Looking for a job or looking for business is a fulltime job. You cannot expect to send out a bunch of letters or register on a job-search site and sit around waiting for the phone to ring. It could happen but it'll take a lot longer – if ever.

Ann Middleman
Westbury, NY
Age, 63

The iceberg exercise

When I first encountered this exercise, I was a student in Georgetown University's Leadership Coaching program. The model was developed by Alexander Caillet (© 2002 Gunn Partners). The premise is that your thoughts affect your feelings; your feelings influence your behaviors; your behaviors manifest as results. At the core of the chain of progression are your beliefs.

The iceberg metaphor works well. Results and behaviors are what we experience or see. Underneath the surface, and the most potentially powerful, are what we cannot see – thoughts, feelings and beliefs.

Example

Current State: You're looking for a job and your resume has done a great job of securing interviews. Yet so far, you have not landed a position. Why not? Let's examine the situation in an "iceberg" view.

The "tip" of the iceberg

- **Results**: Unsuccessful interviews
- **Behaviors:** Projecting an air of desperation and lack of self-confidence. Lackluster answers and performance, including unclear goals, no value proposition (cannot articulate the value that can be provided to the company).

Beneath the surface

- **Feelings:** Depression. Fear. Resignation.

- **Thoughts:** What's the point? They'll probably give the job to some 30-year-old kid anyway.

- **Beliefs:** It's too late for me to get a new job. It's less expensive for companies to hire younger people. I'm too old to start something new.

What if you could change the **beliefs** that underlie everything else? What if, like the donkey in the well, you could view the idea of change as an opportunity instead of a crisis and anticipate success rather than defeat?

Problem...or Opportunity? 21

- Imagine these **beliefs**: "My experiences are valuable. I have unique skills that create additional value."

- Those beliefs might lead to these **thoughts**: "I have a lot to offer this company, but if nothing else, I will make some valuable contacts."

- Those thoughts might engender these **feelings**: optimism, self-confidence, excitement.

- These feelings can lead to more positive **behaviors:** fluid responses, an air of confidence and competence, engaging conversation, attentive body language, a firm handshake, and a reassuring smile.

- And great **results**: a successful interview!

> ### EXERCISE
> On the next page, identify what's going on in your professional life now and what upcoming or recent changes might affect you. (For example, you may have just launched a new business, or you just learned that your company is offering early retirement packages or that your pink slip has just arrived.) Then describe your desired state.
>
> Describe your current state (RESULTS) -- seen above the surface

What BEHAVIORS have you exhibited that support these results?

How are you FEELING?

Describe your THOUGHTS:

_____
_____
_____
_____
_____
_____
_____
_____
_____
_____
_____
_____
_____
_____
_____
_____
_____

What BELIEFS are central to (or at the core of) these thoughts?

_____
_____
_____
_____
_____
_____
_____
_____

> **Now describe your desired RESULTS:**

_____
_____
_____
_____
_____
_____
_____
_____
_____
_____

What BEHAVIORS support these results?

_____
_____
_____
_____
_____
_____
_____
_____
_____
_____
_____
_____
_____
_____
_____
_____

How would you FEEL about these results?

___

Describe your THOUGHTS right now:

What BELIEFS are at the core of these thoughts?

CHAPTER THREE

The Pursuit of Happiness

Copyright, Marva Goldsmith & Associates, Inc

When I really thought about my pursuit, it wasn't about the career or a new business; it was about personal freedom. **I live to be free!**

Ten years ago, I had begun to feel gray, dull, and colorless – like the skies that paint the Detroit winter mornings. My life had taken unexpected turns. My career, though meaningful, was not fulfilling. I felt a need for retooling and reinvention. So I took a leap of faith and went to graduate school.

In plotting your course, the first question you'll need to answer is simply, "What do you want?"

Before you assess where you want to go, it is helpful to take inventory of where you have been. Every moment we've already lived is in the past, so we will call it **"Then."** To begin your journey, you will capture (in Chapter Four) your own personal "Then."

You are on a journey from "Then" to "Now!"

My Own "Then"

Let's confine "Then" to the events and developments of the preceding decade. As an example, here's what my "Then" inventory would look like:

My 40s began this way:

- Great career, but bored and questioning what would be coming next
- Single, without children
- Tired of the harsh winters in Detroit

My 40s ended this way:

- Harvard graduate, entrepreneur, image consultant who literally gets paid to shop; trainer with clients located from coast to coast; member of the International Board of the Association of Image Consultants International (AICI.org); author and public speaker.
- Still single, but happily looking; still without children, but having affected the lives of hundreds (hopefully thousands by the time you read this) of at-risk and incarcerated youth through my workbooks and workshops.
- Escaped the harsh winters of Detroit to a softer, gentler east coast way of living.
- Physically a bit wider and with more gray hairs – but definitely a whole lot wiser!

This is a quick summary to give you an idea of what to record. (I have learned to hit the highlights.) You may want to spend more time on your "Then" story. Let's use Art as an example of what you may want to record…

Art's Story

Then: Corporate Success in the Decade of My 40s

My wife and I were living in our dream house – an 1847 country farmhouse that needed some work and TLC. Thankfully, we still live there today. When I turned 40, our daughter was eight years old and an honor student.

I joined my firm in 1978, when it was a collection of free-thinking individuals working out of the basement of the owner/publisher's home. By 1992, as I entered my 40s, the company published scholarly texts.

I was the boss's right-hand man, overseeing all publishing production operations. I had a good share of executive responsibilities and a large share of IT and telecommunications functions. I had a production staff of 16 and general authority over the entire company.

We were a growing company bursting at the seams, running out of both office and warehouse space at multiple locations.

In 1993 we found a stop-gap solution to our growing pains. I was moved to a building with sufficient warehouse space and just enough office space for the production department. Though just seven miles from the main office, this satellite facility might as well have been light-years away.

Interpersonal communication began to suffer almost immediately after the move. Before, editorial staff could simply walk down the hall to my office to ask a question. Now, they didn't consult, not even by phone. They began making unilateral decisions had detrimental consequences for our publishing program.

The biggest blow, however, came not from corporate operations but from Mother Nature. On Friday, July 8, 1994, massive thunderstorms hammered

Northeastern New Jersey. Our new satellite office was overrun with floodwaters that submerged the parking lot and destroyed seven of our employees' cars. Some of my staff escaped ahead of the flood. A brave few individuals who attempted to wade out were later rescued by volunteers manning rowboats. In the end, I managed to get the remaining eight or nine staff members outside safely and loaded into the back of a tractor trailer, the only vehicle able to make it through the cresting waters as the storm subsided. Like a good captain I stayed, determined to go down with the ship.

We had expanded to the satellite offices only a year before, yet in addition to the problems caused by the flood it was apparent that we were running out of space – again. The good news, at least, was that executive management realized that the dual-office arrangement was unacceptable.

I had no trouble convincing my boss to put me in charge of finding and securing new quarters sufficient to reunite the company – and to move us literally to higher ground!

On July 3, 1995, just a few days shy of the anniversary of the big flood, the production department moved again; this time into our brand-new digs in Mahwah. We were joined by the rest of the company's staff the week following the July 4th holiday.

Our momentous business growth continued. That month we acquired publishing rights to the educational list of a major New York publisher. We next purchased a smaller publishing house and several other additions. We were growing faster than ever before…maybe too fast. Despite our successes, storm clouds had begun to gather. We were always pushing, always trying to accomplish more, and always focusing on growth. This led to some serious job stress.

A few years later, as the millennium approached, a crisis erupted with a key employee; one I had promoted to a top management post during the satellite office days. There were some very serious abuses of power and, more critically and hurtfully, abuses of people.

I had been so involved in general business operations, as well as orchestrating the move to Mahwah, that I simply did not see the problems developing. I also had a serious blind spot with respect to this individual. HR learned of the new manager's abuses through exit interviews with other valuable and talented staff members who had become so disgusted that they chose to quit. Consequently, my boss learned about the abuses, became infuriated, and ultimately forced me to act. The incident caused a rift between me and the manager – a rift that would never fully heal. This was the worst leadership failure in my career.

Around that same time, in 1998, my daughter – my only child – left for college. The empty nest syndrome hit me harder than I could ever have imagined. My wife, now suddenly and almost completely free from the day-to-day responsibilities of parenting, seized the opportunity to ramp up her photography business. I decided to tackle the house restoration projects still to be done. But there I was, surrounded by my saws, hammers and power tools, and wondering, *Why the hell am I doing this?* That's when I realized that I felt very much alone in the world.

I became depressed. I began abusing alcohol which made my depression worse. I came to fear everything. Most of all, despite the fact that at no time in life did I have more "stuff," I developed a chronic and ever-deepening fear of losing everything!

Turning 50: Art's Pinnacle...and His Plunge

I have never seen much point in celebrating my birthday, even the so-called milestone ones. When I walked into my office in 2002 on my 50th birthday, I found 50 boxes of my favorite treat. That was pretty strong evidence that my production staff did not share my view on birthdays. Mallomars were stacked everywhere – on my desk, on the shelves, windowsills – everywhere. It was an auspicious beginning to my 50s. The Mallomars were evidence that "my people" both respected and, for the most part, liked me. I always tried to be a compassionate manager and mentor and to protect my staff when they made honest mistakes. They seemed to have forgiven my major error in judgment about the abusive manager, and for the previous seven years I had retained all of my book production editors. In many respects, these were the pinnacle years of my publishing career. I had a great staff and the respect of my peers. My daughter graduated from college and came home again. Things should have been getting better, but unfortunately, I still had persistent, underlying personal problems.

In late spring of 2003, my boss called me into his office. He swore me to confidence, confessing his decision to sell the company. At first I did not believe him; he had talked about selling before. But, when he told me this time, I was convinced that he meant it. He said he had lost the drive and lost the "fire in his belly" for this business. This was a highly competitive man who, if he could not do something well enough to compete, would not do it at all. I knew he was done.

He also asked me to resign from the company. It was largely my own fault. While I had made some progress taming my personal demons, even in the midst of professional success my depressive moods and my sometimes erratic performance were burdens he could no longer afford – not as he focused on selling the company. I tendered my resignation on July 31.

In the days leading up to my departure I tried to stay positive. I even fantasized walking out of the office on that last Friday afternoon and feeling the "lifting" of that great and proverbial "weight from my shoulders" that we so often hear about. But my real experience was nothing of the sort.

Instead, on that next Monday, at the age of 53, I was unemployed for the first time in my life. Despite my very generous 18-month severance package, I was in a state of utter panic, consumed with an irrational need to find a new job *immediately*. I set out on a frantic but fruitless job search that lasted nearly three years.

Then one day I changed my mind. I decided, *Let's change course.*

And I wasn't alone. The company sold a year and a half later for $71 million, putting most of the 100 remaining employees out of work.

Turning 50: Art's "Road Not Taken"

> "When you come to a fork in the road, take it!"
> – Yogi Berra

In my final days with the company, I had thought about trying to land a production director position with a small university press. My thinking was this: something nonprofit, university subsidized, with a little less stress, a lot less emphasis on making profit, and a smaller, more manageable workload. I saw myself wearing one of those corduroy sport jackets with the patches on the elbows, walking around a quaint university town in Hush Puppies®, looking like a psychology professor. Maybe I'd even take up pipe smoking to complete the look. My impression was that university press positions were highly prized and immensely fulfilling – after all, they published important stuff, even if some of it was rather obscure. Well... that was then.

Recently, one of these "ideal" positions actually came open. I pounced. I soon received a call from the director of the press to schedule a conference call interview with the search committee. "I believe I'm the first candidate he's called," I told myself. "I believe I am in."

In the days leading up to the interview, with three years of perspective since having left my life in the corporate world, I began to have second thoughts – serious second thoughts. Did I really want to go back to what I had done for nearly 30 years? Did I really want to go back to doing something I could probably do in my sleep? What would happen if they actually offered me this job? Was it *truly* what I wanted now? I realized that something deep within me had really, almost pervasively, changed.

Subconsciously, these thoughts must have weighed heavily on me; I blew the interview big time. I was simply not myself. I was nervous; I vacillated; I rambled. To my horror, we somehow got off on a discussion of my worst leadership failure – *at length.* I still have no idea exactly how that happened, but I remember feeling powerless to regain control of the conversation.

Bye-bye elbow patches

So what exactly changed during those three years? First, I gained control over my problem with alcohol. Without that, no progress would have been possible.

Second, I survived three years of unemployment – long enough to know that there is indeed life after corporate. I am still here, still living in my now (nearly!) refurbished farmhouse, still married to a woman who adores me, and the proud father of my daughter, who's now a 28-year-old woman.

Third, I lost my fear. At 56, my journey has led me to control. I now control fear; fear does not control me. The most joyful part is that I have recaptured the very confidence that enabled me to join a start-up company way back when I began this journey.

I realized that what I wanted was a challenge. And something else – I realized that there was something I have wanted to do since I was 12, something I repressed for 40 years: **I want to write**. That is my answer to the first question addressed in this book. "What do you want?" **I want to write**. I also know that to get from "Then" to "Now" will take hard work.

Art: confident, prepared for the challenge, resilient, skilled, creative, and loved.

Coach's Check-In

Did anything in Art's story resonate with you? Could this have been a chapter in your book? Do you know others with the same story? It is interesting to note that when Art went to the interview for what he thought was his "dream job," his heart was not in it.

What was he thinking? What was he feeling? How did it manifest in his behaviors? If you did not complete the **Iceberg Exercise***, now is the time.*

At this point in our lives, we are looking for work that makes our hearts sing. If we have the luxury of discovery, we will find or create an opportunity in which the heart sings and our bills are paid. This is indeed the ultimate opportunity.

EXERCISE

> Take this time to begin creating that opportunity for yourself. Capture in writing the thoughts that Art's story stirred up for you. You'll need them as we go along!

_____
_____
_____
_____
_____
_____
_____
_____
_____
_____
_____
_____
_____
_____
_____
_____
_____
_____
_____
_____
_____
_____
_____
_____

Create the change you want to see: Using the SWOT analysis as a personal inventory

Harlan David "Colonel" Sanders began building his Kentucky Fried Chicken Empire at the age of 65.

It is never too late to start a second career – to move from "Then" to "Now." So how does Art go about branding himself as a writer at the age of 56?

Art acknowledged that the main requirement would be hard work. He's right. So let's get started with a deeper assessment of the product, which in this case is **Art**. We will conduct a SWOT analysis. SWOT is an acronym for Strengths, Weaknesses, Opportunities, and Threats. You can use the SWOT analysis to help identify and document your personal pluses and minuses:

SWOT

INTERNAL

STRENGTHS

WEAKNESSES

EXTERNAL

OPPORTUNITIES

THREATS

Art's SWOT

Strengths
- Excellent command of the English language, with a strong vocabulary and writing skills
- Maturity and experience from 30 years in scholarly publishing, yet fresh and up-to-date
- Ability to remain impartial; to see the merit and the folly of all sides of an issue or a story

- Adept at constructing and presenting strong, logical, and persuasive arguments from multiple perspectives; capable of recognizing, respecting, and understanding opposing viewpoints

Weaknesses
- Self-doubt about being able to make a living, particularly in the short term, so that I can segue from my temporary retail job without "losing the farm." I imagine a crystallizing moment when I can calmly, and with immense satisfaction, tender my resignation to the department store because my income from writing has surpassed that from retail, and I can focus all of my attention and energies in that direction.
- Another aspect of self-doubt – the knowledge that it will be very hard work to build a gainful writing career while having to work full time at a mind numbing, spirit-sapping occupation scares the hell out of me.

Opportunities
- Limitless – registered on one freelance Internet site that seems to post 20–30 new opportunities every day, and that's only one site; have current *Writer's Marketplace* with listings of over 3,500 publishers or places to publish
- Range – the beauty of writing is that it can be applied to anything from advertising to business to culture to art to history to current affairs

Threats
- Personal energy – It will be draining to get my writing career off the ground while I'm tethered to a full-time job for the health insurance and income it provides. I feel fairly positive about this, as the combination of fervent desire and financial necessity make for a powerful dual force to make it happen.

In My Experience...

On December 31, 2009, the Company completed a global corporate cost take-out initiative; in plain language, I was laid off. The European-based Corporation applied a corporate mandate to each Country and sliced major costs to properly size its operating base. During the same time, the Company posted record earnings and it continues to prosper.

I was the IT Project Lead on a 3-year project that was sponsored by a key executive who left the company half way through the project. Before leaving, the sponsor stated that those who participated on this high velocity (long hour initiative) would be recognized as leading the company through the transformation. (Unfortunately, *recognized* must have meant **laid off**.)

Three months prior to the actual severance date, I become aware that my future with the company was not a long term prospect. So, I began looking for work early in the game. I spent 6 months, 12-14 hours/day (plus weekends) networking and investigating how to get ahead of the millions of others also looking for jobs. I quickly realized through conversations with recruiters and my own findings that employers are swamped with resumes and sometimes posted job requirements change (become narrowly focused) after reviewing hundreds of resumes with similar qualifications. Additionally, employers are attempting to roll requirements for many legacy job descriptions into one position –to reduce the IT cost footprint.

Network, network, network is to the job search as location, location, location is to real estate. I landed my position through traditional networking as the employer was looking for specific skills (Enterprise Architecture) that I had picked up at my last employer. I was well qualified for what they were looking for and I nailed all interview questions/ discussions – even bringing to light additional value I could provide on top of what they required.

There is an element of street smarts and valued-legacy mindset that exists in the over 50's workforce that is nearly impossible to replace. Unfortunately, not all organizations realize or evaluate based on that criteria.

To what specifically do you attribute your success? Persistence and not getting emotional; head down, long hours – old fashioned qualities that are attributed to Baby Boomers – and hard work .

What lessons or insights would you share with others in a similar position? Don't take anything for granted. There is no such thing as "30 and out" anymore.

How is your new job different from what you have done in the past, if at all? Much of the work is the same, but there is less stress with a more realistic timetable than my last project. I feel much better. I have my life back! Previously, I traveled 100% for nearly three years – only to be laid off.

Steve Letsinger
Lake Orion, MI
Age 58

Coach's Check-In

Know yourself. Know your customer. Then, you can easily articulate the value that you can bring to the customer (employer).

CHAPTER FOUR

So, What Do You Want?

Who are you in the Market Place?

Copyright, Marva Goldsmith & Associates, Inc

Establishing your brand identity

Your first step on the journey of recharging your personal brand after age 50 is to begin writing your "Then" statement. Ask yourself all sorts of open-ended questions like these:

- How do you see yourself and your accomplishments over the past ten years?
- What would you say were the defining moments in your life during that time?
- What major decisions have you (or others) made that affected you?
- What led you to the path you have been on?

- Is it your joy in life to walk this path, or is this road one that is paved by necessity or responsibility?
- What are your major accomplishments or your life challenges?
- What changes occurred over the last decade?

Answering these questions will help to define "Then" for you just as Art and I did in Chapter Three.

Coach's Check-In

Before we move on, I did mention that this is an action guide, right? The operative word is "**action**."

You have read Art's story and reviewed his SWOT analysis in Chapter Three. This chapter is all about you!

To begin plotting your path, capture in writing your own personal "Then" inventory and SWOT analysis.

EXERCISE

Are you warmed up yet?

I described Art's attributes as confident, prepared for the challenge, resilient, skilled, creative, and loved. What specific attributes can you use to describe yourself? If you are unsure, consider taking the personal brand assessment on my website (branding50.com). The assessment provides a thorough examination of how you are perceived by others.

___

Art described his goal succinctly: **"I want to write."** What are your goals for this branding exercise? What do you hope to accomplish?

List up to three goals. The more succinctly you can list your goals, the easier it will be to work towards them.

___

Your SWOT

With your goal(s) in mind, complete your own SWOT analysis using the spaces provided on the following pages, on a separate sheet of paper, or in a journal or notebook. (You have my permission to make copies of these SWOT exercises.)

Self-assessment is never easy. Ask friends, relatives, and co-workers to help you identify your strengths and weaknesses. Consider copying the following pages and asking others to give you an honest appraisal. You might be surprised at what other people think your strengths and weaknesses are. Have fun with these exercises as you engage others in your work.

This is also a good time to take a few online assessments (Strengths Finder, Myers-Briggs, Keirsey Temperament, etc.). These assessments may also help you articulate your strengths and weaknesses. Take the Reach Personal Branding Assessment. Visit Branding50.com for special offers.

STRENGTHS

Your internal **Strengths** include your inherent abilities, your skills, your qualifications and credentials – all the things that you can control that can help you attain your goals.

_____
_____
_____
_____
_____
_____
_____
_____
_____
_____
_____
_____

WEAKNESSES

Your internal **Weaknesses** are the things that control you; things that will hold you back from attaining your goals unless you address them head on. Your weaknesses may include a lack of certain skills or abilities, a disposition that is inherently negative (glass half-empty mentality), or the lack of certain credentials needed to reach your goals. The key here is to identify the weakness and make changes to impact, minimize or eradicate them.

_____

_____

_____

_____

_____

_____

_____

_____

_____

Opportunities and **Threats** are external forces that can either help or hinder you from reaching your goals. Think globally, especially as you describe your opportunities and threats.

OPPORTUNITIES

Are there **Opportunities** presented by technology or the Internet that can help you reach your goals? How are you capitalizing on the explosion of social networking opportunities such as Facebook, Twitter, LinkedIn, and a galaxy of other tools that are literally at your fingertips? What networking vehicles or blogs are available within your industry? And don't try to tell me that stuff is "just for kids" because you'd be surprised how many grandparents rely on the Internet today to keep in touch with their far-flung families. If you ignore the fact that this is how millions of people communicate these days, you're missing the boat. Get on board and get online! (See Addendum on this subject)

Think past your immediate base of friends and family; who is in your network that can assist you? More importantly, think about *how* they might be of help. Do you know others who have achieved goals similar to yours? Who else is doing what you want to do – and doing it well? What gates did they open? What did they have to overcome to reach this goal?

_____
_____
_____
_____
_____
_____
_____
_____
_____
_____

THREATS

What are the external **Threats** that may derail you from achieving your goals? In this economy, it is easy to identify once unforeseen threats – stock market collapse, housing collapse, recession, downsizing and a host of other maladies that have plagued the country. Try to make this section more personal. What threats are close to home for you as you peer into the future?

_____
_____
_____
_____
_____
_____
_____
_____

Unique selling proposition: Your sweet spot

The information you gather and document by doing the SWOT exercise can help you formulate what is called your *unique selling proposition* (USP).

The unique selling proposition is the implicit promise that you are providing to your clients, prospects, or potential employers (your "target") in exchange for them doing business with you or hiring or promoting you. But, do you know what your Unique Selling Proposition (USP) is?

Here are a few examples of commercial products that offered unique selling propositions:

- Head & Shoulders: "Gets rid of dandruff"
- Visine: "Gets the red out"
- FedEx: "When your package absolutely, positively has to get there overnight"
- Kentucky Fried Chicken: "Finger lickin' good"
- M&Ms: "Milk chocolate that melts in your mouth, not in your hand"

A USP is a distinct idea that distinguishes you and/or your business from every other competitor. It is developed for each target market. It answers the question, "What value can you provide to your target that will help solve a problem, increase market share, or improve business, etc.?" You want to focus on that one niche, need, or gap that is lacking for your target – provided you can keep the promise you make to the client or your employer.

In My Experience...

You may have read the headlines when it occurred on September 13, 2002: Hewlett-Packard Company bought Compaq. I was Global I.T. Manager when I received my lay-off notice.

I had put away some savings and bought some investment property but still, the separation was scary. I was never bitter about being let go, but I understand being laid off can elicit feelings of anger and bitterness. I think you have to limit the time you spend dwelling in that place.

With the job market as tight as it was in Northern Colorado, I looked around for two months and considered moving out of state for a job. But with two teenage daughters in school and a wife who was a teacher in the community, I was reluctant to uproot my family after seven years in Fort Collins, Colorado. Having previously lived in San Francisco and Bristol, England, when I was with HP, the family had done some traveling but we liked Northern Colorado and wanted to stay. That is when I realized I needed to make something happen myself.

First, I had to stop feeling sorry for myself – and look at the current circumstances as a VERY POSITIVE, EXCITING, and CHALLENGING new opportunity. That's when I decided to start my own consulting business: Levy Consulting, LLC and NorthernColoradoRentals.com, LLC.

NorthernColoradoRentals.com was a web-based rental property listing service. My partner and I started out by asking for an endorsement from the largest real estate company in Northern Colorado, The Group, Inc. Once we got that endorsement we visited the largest property management companies in Northern Colorado, selling them on our value proposition versus their continuing to advertise in the local newspaper. We were able to easily convince them that we would be 1/10th the cost and five times more effective than newspaper classified advertising. In order to initially build up enough volume, we offered everyone one month of FREE listings. From there we were able to continually increase our momentum. We were cash flow positive after 30 days, and we recouped our initial investment after just six months.

Clearly the most successful strategy we employed was "networking" with key individuals within our **target market**– specifically, the largest real estate company and the largest property management companies in our area.

People learned about us mostly through "networking" and "word of mouth." We also joined the local apartment association (Northern Colorado Rental Housing Association) and the local chapter of NARPM (National Association of Residential Property Managers). We conducted quite a bit of SEO (Search Engine Optimization) on our website so that people would easily find us through the various internet search engines (e.g. Google).

To what specifically do you attribute your success? There were four primary keys to our success:

1. POSITIVE ATTITUDE: a personal drive to be successful no matter what and then the discipline to stay focused on the key elements that would lead to making the business successful.
2. UNWAVERING FOCUS ON CUSTOMER SERVICE & CUSTOMER SATISFACTION: When we first went into full operation, I'd wake up every morning, go downstairs to my home office, and hope that there would be emails or phone calls from upset customers. I knew that I could easily turn an unhappy customer into a very satisfied customer in less than five minutes – and then that customer would probably be a customer for life and tell 10-100 of his/her friends about us.
3. Creating a very easy to explain and understand VALUE PROPOSITION for our customers. We made it very simple: We were going to be 1/10th the cost and at least five times more effective than any other alternative form of advertising.
4. Setting up the entire business to easily TRACK METRICS and STATISTICS on a daily, weekly, monthly, and annual basis. For example, we were able to easily track the effectiveness of where we spent our own advertising dollars to promote our website business. So, we know exactly how much it costs to get a new customer by advertising on the backs of city bus benches versus advertising in a newspaper or by using Google Adwords online which enables us to make key business & financial investment decisions.

Is there anything else that you want to share with others...words of wisdom? If you decide to start your own business, make sure you do the following when you start out:

- Stay focused on the operational details. Have an action plan with due dates. Don't get distracted. Stay focused on the critical success factors. Focus on the 80% that is most important and let the other 20% go.
- Focus on when you will become "cash flow positive" and when you will "recoup your initial investment."

- Have someone who is focusing on marketing and sales. It doesn't matter how great the product or service is if nobody knows about it or what VALUE it brings to the customer.

  Michael Levy
  Fort Collins, CO
  Age: 55

Coach's Check-In

Selecting a narrow niche allows you to focus your resources and become known to a target audience. This applies to new business owners as well as job hunters.

> *EXERCISE*
> Develop your unique selling proposition.

Step 1: Identify your most compelling benefits.

With the needs of your target in mind, describe the three most compelling benefits you or your company can offer your target market. Explain WHY this benefit is important to the target. Think about the result that your client (or potential employer) desires from you, your product, or your service.

_____
_____
_____
_____
_____
_____
_____
_____

Step 2: What makes you (or your offer, product, or service) unique?

No two people have the exact same skills, experiences, or abilities. Therefore, there is a unique quality in your personal brand. It is your challenge to define it and package it for a target market (employer or client base).

Step 3: Solve a "pain point" for someone.

Before an interview, research the company and the industry to ensure that you understand what is causing pain for the target. Yes, pain! The key to marketing any product or service is to find a need and fill it. In the following examples, identify the pain point.

Company	USP	Pain Point
Head & Shoulders	"Gets rid of your dandruff"	Dandruff is socially unacceptable.
Visine	"Gets the red out"	
FedEx	"When your package absolutely, positively has to get there overnight"	
Kentucky Fried Chicken	"Finger lickin' good"	
M&Ms	"Milk chocolate that melts in your mouth, not in your hand"	
Others?		

In My Experience...

I had been Director of Conferences for Educom, a non-profit association in Washington, D.C., for a number of years. In 1998, the organization merged with CAUSE to form EDUCAUSE. Staying with the new organization would have required that I relocate to Boulder, CO, which was not a desirable choice for me, so my husband and I took this opportunity to move to Florida.

When I first moved to Florida, I worked for a while as a freelance meeting planner. I also joined several newcomers groups in Sarasota, learned to play bridge, and settled into "retirement." After a few years of this activity, I knew I needed to find something more meaningful. I knew that whatever was next for me would need to involve the things I most enjoy, and over time I conceived the idea of a new business that would provide assistance to seniors who are moving.

One of the most valuable things I did was to seek the counsel of the local Small Business Development Center. They provided supportive mentors who helped me develop both a marketing plan and a business plan. To find new clients, I did a lot of targeted networking, and made it my business to meet as many people as possible who could refer business to me.

Since starting my business in 2007, I have assisted almost one hundred families with the moves of elderly family members; either to a smaller home or into a retirement or assisted living community. My services include helping them decide what to take with them, packing and unpacking, finding and supervising a mover, hanging pictures, and disposing of the items they no longer need. We provide very caring emotional support for our clients in addition to our detail-oriented logistical support (visit: ww.myseniormoves.com). My success is largely due to the delivery of caring, quality service to my clients and to consistent networking.

What lessons or insights would you share with others in a similar position? First, answer the questions: What is your passion? What are you good at doing? What do you love to do? Then, find a business that matches your skills and passion. Since opening Senior Moves, I have developed a new sense of self-worth, and a greater degree of self-confidence.

What advice would you give or did you receive that was most helpful throughout the changes you made? You are never too old to find and follow your passion.

Is there anything else that you want to share with others...words of wisdom? You may find that some of your friends pull away from you as you embark on a new course. They will feel threatened and perhaps a little envious. Don't let this stop you from following your passion.

Sue Ellen Addicott
Sarasota, FL
Age: 64

ENHANCED VISIBILITY: Sue Ellen can be heard on Senior Savvy Radio WTMY 1280 (or wtmy.com) on Saturdays from noon to 1:00 PM EST)

Who are your targets and what causes them pain? How can you specifically address the targets' needs?

TARGET	Target's Pain Point	Unique Selling Proposition
SENIOR MOVES: *A senior who is downsizing or moving to assisted living*	*The transition from independent living to assisted living or to a nursing home can be overwhelming.*	*Experienced logistics professional provides caring emotional support and relocation services for seniors who are moving and for their families.*

Step 4: Prove it!

What evidence supports your claim that you can deliver on your unique selling proposition? Cite examples, stories, relevant experiences, and credentials.

Your Unique Selling Proposition	Proof Points
SENIOR MOVES: *Experienced logistics professional provides caring emotional support and relocation services for seniors who are moving and for their families.*	*Since 2007, Senior Moves has assisted one hundred families with the moves of elderly family members.*

Step 5: Now develop a Yellow Pages ad that tells the story.

Review the previous pages. Start with your main target (you can develop several ads). First, write a statement that incorporates all of the elements (target, pain points, USP, and proof).

Senior Moves: For senior citizens who are downsizing or moving to assisted living and their adult children who are unable to assist with the move (target), Senior Moves has reduced the stress and anxiety (pain points) for hundreds of seniors (proof point) by reinventing home on a smaller scale with care, emotional support, detail-oriented logistical expertise and a designer's touch (USP).

Marva Goldsmith: For Baby Boomers (target) in the midst of career transition (pain points), I use my personal experience of reinvention from engineer to brand coach (proof point), coupled with creativity, drive and a collaborative approach to develop personal brand strategies that help find jobs, secure contracts, and achieve more professional success (USP).

_____
_____
_____
_____
_____
_____
_____
_____
_____
_____
_____
_____
_____
_____
_____
_____
_____

You can also use variations of your yellow pages ad in your marketing collateral and, in some cases, a brief, toned-down version on your résumé.

Remove the Stress and Anxiety from your Move to Senior Living

Are you downsizing or moving to assisted living? Do you live too far away to assist your elderly parents with their big move? Rely on Senior Moves to reinvent home on a smaller scale. From packing to hanging those sentimental pictures, our logistical team will manage the minutest detail with care, compassion and a designer's touch!

Baby Boomer Meets Personal Branding

Marva Goldsmith can help you reinvent your career, because she has lived it! At age 42, she reinvented herself from a mid-level executive in the utility industry to become a certified image professional, brand coach, and speaker. She works with mid-career professionals to help them find jobs, secure contracts, and achieve more professional success by applying commercial branding techniques to their reinvention efforts.

Use this exercise to develop your own "brand advertising" that will excite you and gain the interest of your target audience. Most importantly, a powerful USP will act as a compelling force to inspire consistent delivery on your brand promise.

_____

_____

_____

_____

_____

_____

_____

_____

CHAPTER FIVE

Branding: What It Is... and What It Ain't

Ketchup

Tomatoes + spices + high fructose corn syrup = ketchup. Right? Pretty much. For the most part we can agree that all brands of ketchup are made of essentially the same ingredients. So, how does one brand distinguish itself from all the other ketchup bottles on the shelf?

Heinz captures more than 40 percent of the ketchup market by branding itself based on a single attribute: it's thick. What can we learn about branding ourselves, or our small businesses, from the Heinz ketchup example? Through several successful ad campaigns, Heinz has become known as the slow, thick, rich ketchup. Do you remember any of the following?

Tagline: "Worth the Wait"
Ad copy: "Slowest ketchup in the West"
(See it on youtube.com)
Ad song: "Anticipation" by Carly Simon

The packaging is now designed to accommodate this well-established attribute. Heinz changed the orientation of the bottle such that it is stored upside down – still rich and thick, but now, no waiting.

Can you accept that in the workplace (or the marketplace) you are no different than ketchup? No matter what you do – trainer, HR specialist, engineer, teacher – there are many other people who essentially do the same thing and have similar credentials (or ingredients) as you. So, what attributes make you different and special in your marketplace? Keep in mind that Heinz does not go after everyone who likes ketchup. Its target market is just those consumers who prefer thicker, heartier ketchup. If you like soupy or runny ketchup, you won't reach for Heinz.

It is important to understand that "distinguishing yourself" does not mean you are the only person in your organization, or marketplace, with these attributes. Heinz is not the only thick, hearty ketchup on the shelf. They were just the first to use this unique selling proposition, and now they have the brand distinction of being "the slow ketchup," or the "thicker ketchup." In branding yourself, you are simply pointing out how *you want* to be characterized.

What is personal branding?

We should start with a conversation about what personal branding is NOT. I once ran across a great list on a website belonging to Tom Peters, who is credited with starting the phenomenon of personal branding, with his article "The Brand Called YOU," which was featured in the magazine *Fast Company* in 1997.

The author of the annotated list is Rajesh Setty:

- **IT'S NOT** what you say about yourself. Your personal brand is an assessment the marketplace makes about who you are and what you bring to the marketplace.
- **IT'S NOT** an extension of your employer's brand – unless you are self-employed.
- **IT'S NOT** your presence in social media. Social media can amplify your personal brand, but your presence there is not a substitute for a personal brand – unless you're a social media expert.
- **IT'S NOT** about the power alone. Power and influence are just possible side benefits of your personal brand. Personal branding is about what you can give to the world.
- **IT'S NOT** a gift that someone can give you. But they can give you a gift to amplify an "already powerful" personal brand – a well-deserved link, an endorsement, a testimonial, etc.
- **IT'S NOT** permanent. It's not something that you can get and keep it for life. Just as you must intentionally develop a powerful personal brand, you have to continue to provide meaningful action in order to maintain and grow that brand.
- **A PERSONAL BRAND IS** your promise to the market-place and the world. Everyone has a personal brand. The real question is whether someone's personal brand is powerful enough to be meaningful to the person and the marketplace.

"Personal branding is an identity that stimulates precise, meaningful perceptions in its audience about the values and qualities the person stands for."
– Peter Montoya, author, personal branding expert

"Personal branding is [simply] a way to clarify and communicate what makes you different and special; then use those qualities to guide your business and career decisions."
– William Arruda, author, personal branding expert

Just like the Heinz brand, we must establish a leadership role in our field. We must stand out from all of the other ketchup bottles on the shelf. One of the most effective ways of strengthening a brand is to narrow the focus. **Think: Starbucks, Toys-R-Us, Subway.** No doubt there are hundreds of attributes you could use to describe You, Incorporated. To strengthen your brand, to distinguish yourself from all the other ketchup bottles on the shelf, you need to determine the "top of mind" response people have when they think of you. What words best describe your leadership role? For example: Volvo is described by two attributes: safety and luxury. Heinz is the thicker, richer ketchup.

The most difficult part of personal branding is to identify your leadership role – what makes you different and special. What do you want to be known for?

The next exercise should help you articulate those distinguishing characteristics.

> *EXERCISE*
> Make four copies of the next page. (You have my permission.) Circle all the attributes that describe you. Now distill the list into three attributes that you consider the most important. These are your key features.

For a more in-depth analysis of your brand, take the 360° web-based personal brand assessment on my website. It will help you understand how you are perceived by those around you. It gives you the critical feedback you need so you can expand your career or business success. It's an integral part of the personal branding process and an indispensable tool for thriving in today's professional environment. Visit branding50.com

PERSONAL BRAND ATTRIBUTES

- Accessible
- Accomplished
- Accurate
- Active
- Adaptable
- Adventurous
- Aggressive
- Aloof
- Arrogant
- Ambitious
- Analytical
- Assertive
- Beautiful
- Bold
- Charismatic
- Charming
- Cheerful
- Collaborative
- Community-oriented
- Competitive
- Confident
- Connected
- Conservative
- Controlling
- Creative
- Curious
- Dependable
- Detail oriented
- Devoted
- Diplomatic
- Driven
- Dramatic
- Dynamic
- Easygoing
- Efficient
- Eloquent
- Empathetic
- Energetic
- Enthusiastic
- Entrepreneurial
- Ethical
- Extroverted
- Flexible
- Forceful
- Formal
- Friendly
- Funny
- Generous
- Giving
- Healthy
- Helpful
- Honest
- Humble
- Humorous
- Imaginative
- Inventive
- Sophisticated
- Self-motivated
- Impatient
- Insensitive
- Intelligent
- Introverted
- Intense
- Inspiring
- Intuitive
- Kind-hearted
- Likable
- Loyal
- Loving
- Materialistic
- Melodramatic
- Methodical
- Modest
- Moody
- Motivating
- Open-minded
- Optimistic
- Organized
- Original
- Outgoing
- Passionate
- Persuasive
- Philanthropic
- Physically Fit
- Procrastinating
- Productive
- Professional
- Quick-Witted
- Receptive
- Refined
- Relentless
- Reliable
- Religious
- Resourceful
- Responsive
- Risk taking
- Ruthless
- Savvy
- Self-assured
- Sincere
- Sophisticated
- Shy
- Socially-conscious
- Spoiled
- Spiritual
- Strategic
- Stubborn
- Successful
- Supportive
- Thoughtful
- Tolerant
- Trusting
- Trustworthy
- Unflappable
- Versatile
- Visionary
- Witty
- Wise
- Worldly

_____
_____
_____
_____
_____
_____
_____
_____
_____
_____
_____
_____
_____
_____
_____
_____
_____
_____
_____
_____

I hope you followed the instructions to make four copies of the previous page. Now, ask four trusted colleagues to circle up to six attributes that best describe you. (Sorry, we're working in the business domain, so you can't ask your mother or your spouse.)

Write their responses in the chart on the next page. Circle any attribute cited by more than one person. The more circles you see with the same or similar meaning, the better (assuming the items circled are attributes you *want* associated with your brand). That means you have at least been consistent in the image you project.

Underline any circled attributes that were on your list of key attributes. Ideally, your colleagues have written all or most of the attributes that you identified during your self-assessment.

Coach's Check-In

What themes did your colleagues identify? Were there any surprises? Sometimes we find that we have to live up to the perception held by others: other people see attributes in us that we do not realize are present.

If your colleagues picked different attributes from each other and from your self-assessment, you need to think about the consistency of your message. But don't worry: this is important information you can use to improve the branding of You, Incorporated. (Of course, you can contact MG&A for brand coaching, too.)

What distinguishes me from others in my field?

Colleague 1	Colleague 2	Colleague 3	Colleague 4

A simple way to brand yourself – whether you are an entrepreneur or an employee looking to rise above the fray – is to establish a leadership role in your field, gain visibility for the leadership role, and be consistent in your approach to deliver on your brand promise.

Dennis Rodman: A Unique Personal Brand

How do we create ourselves as a brand? Remember former NBA star Dennis Rodman? We can use him as an example of ingenious – and absolutely unique – personal branding. I have used the "Rodman brand" to demonstrate the power of personal branding in my workshops since 2005 because his brand is both unforgettable and highly visible. When he was just a nondescript 5'11" high school kid, Rodman didn't even play basketball, but after graduation he grew eight inches and joined a college team. Over the years he transformed himself, developing the Dennis Rodman brand into what his NBA.com bio calls "one of the most recognized athletes in the world...." Rodman was a defensive superstar in the NBA for 14 years (NBA.com called him "arguably the best rebounding forward in NBA history"), but even people who care nothing about the sport often recognize his name and can usually tell you something about him.

What does that mean? It means that when we think of Dennis Rodman, there are two or three words (besides dominant rebounder and defender) that thousands of people associate with him: **Outrageous Bad Boy.**

Rodman and leadership

Rodman was a leader in his marketplace, the National Basketball Association; a rebounder who would stop at nothing to get the ball and one of the best rebounders in the history of the game – and he has five championship rings to back up the claim.

Rodman and visibility

What Rodman did brilliantly, and in a most unconventional way, was gain visibility. He started changing his appearance both on and off the court; constantly altering his hair color, flashing multiple tattoos, and displaying numerous body piercings. His metamorphosis from Dennis Rodman of the Detroit Pistons to Dennis Rodman of the Chicago Bulls was headline news on both the sports and entertainment pages. He became a celebrity and began to appear on talk shows – not because he was a fierce rebounder (although that helped), but because of his outrageous behavior and eccentric appearance. Being extreme is what made him different, notable, and very *special*.

Rodman and consistency

To brand yourself in a way that's understood by all, you must be consistent in your message. Rodman was consistent, both on the court as well as off the court. During the 90s when he was a part of the championship Pistons and championship Bulls teams, he became more infamous for his antics on and off the court than for his undeniable playing abilities. That was his goal and he was rewarded.

Ultimately, successful branding leads to a purchase or a decision. It certainly did in Rodman's case. He made movies, appeared on reality TV shows, and wrote two bestselling books. My favorite demonstration of brand strength is the commercial he made for milk producers. Wearing a milk mustache, and with his buff chest bared, Rodman sent a message without saying a word. Why would producers of such a wholesome product as milk hire Dennis Rodman? Because their message was clear: **Even Bad Boys Drink Milk!**

Although Rodman left professional basketball in 2000, the Dennis Rodman brand continues to resurface, including when he appeared in the 2009 season of *Celebrity Apprentice*, a reality TV show produced by Donald Trump. Why Rodman, when he's no longer in the NBA? Because of his brand: he consistently delivers on Brand Promise. The producers knew that Rodman, just by showing up, would boost the show's ratings.

Other successful personal brands

Love them or not, there are many historical and current examples of successful, powerful personal brands in business (Henry Ford, Bill Gates, Oprah, Warren Buffet), government (Franklin Roosevelt, Ronald Reagan, Barack Obama), and every other facet of life (from Mother Jones to Mother Teresa). It's not necessary to be outrageous, as Rodman is (that's *his* brand), only to demonstrate what makes you different in your "marketplace." You must own a leadership role and be acknowledged for it.

Gaining visibility for that role may be as simple as positioning yourself as an expert by writing a few articles or maintaining a blog.

In My Experience...

After nearly 50 years (combined) in private practice as psychotherapists, specializing in relationship work with couples and singles, we were ready for something else. In addition to our practice, we conducted a lot of speaking and corporate consultation and conducted weekend seminars.

We had wanted to move from Los Angeles for a number of years. So we shut down our practices in 2000 and moved to a charming little town in upstate New York, Windham. Our new home was way out in the country and we supported ourselves with a radio show for Wisdom Radio that we hosted from home. We loved every minute of the move and have never looked back.

While still in Los Angeles we negotiated the contract for our third book, *Be Loved For You Really Are*, and took the work of writing the book with us to Windham.

In early 2005, we discovered Internet marketing and came online with our work. Initially we just marketed our programs and products to the people on our email lists. As we grew our online business, we did more and more joint venture promotions with other people who were also growing their online businesses and who were in related fields.

In our first year online we only grossed $32,000. By 2008, when we produced our first two "Bridging Heart and Marketing" conferences – which were promoted exclusively online – we grossed $238,000. And we've been in the 6 figures ever since.

The radio show arrangement had come to an end before we got involved online so our success online has been largely through affiliate and joint venture promotions. We have a membership site - Soft Sell Marketers Association (our members have joined primarily through our conferences). We also offer website analysis for our list members, and miscellaneous product sales that come from a variety of sources like article marketing. We went from being psychotherapists to Internet marketers who created and promoted our own relationship programs, which followed easily since we are best-selling authors of four relationship books. But finding combat-driven, hard-sell marketing offensive and damaging to the potential customer, we soon saw the need to develop our own style of soft sell copywriting which we taught and now market as a home study course htttp://softtopiccopywritingsecrets.com

That was followed by the awareness that our soft sell service provider audience needed their own marketing conference so we produced "Bridging Heart and Marketing" conferences to instruct others in the soft sell marketing approach. Then we established the Soft Sell Marketers Association, an international hub for the growth and success of soft sell marketers' businesses http://softsellmarketersassorciation.org.

And now through our #1 bestselling book *The Heart of Marketing -- Love Your Customers and They Will Love You Back* (Morgan James Publishing, May 2009) we are inspiring an ever larger audience to create a soft sell heart-based platform for their businesses. BTW, we knew our Soft Sell Marketing brand was needed and wanted when people told us that our first conference (February 2008) would be a failure and we would lose a fortune. Instead, we had over 100 people attend from all over the United States, Denmark, Australia, and Canada and we came out with a very nice profit and testimonials of gratitude from dozens of the participants.

What lessons or insights would you share with others in a similar position?

Know that age has nothing to do with it – seize the opportunity to reinvent yourself and go for it!

How is your new career different from what you have done in the past, if at all?

Our new job is totally different - EXCEPT that we're now using our relationship expertise to teach and promote Soft Sell Marketing - Bridging Heart and Marketing!

What are the largest changes that have occurred as a result of your new position?

After coming online with no technical skills or background in marketing or selling we have become professional marketers. AND, we know if we can do it in our 60s then most people can do whatever it is they want!

Is there anything else that you want to share with others...words of wisdom?

Use the new opportunity to grow. Expand your Heart. Listen to your Soul. Go Forward with everything you've got!

Husband and wife:
Judith Sherven, PhD (Age, 66)
Jim Sniechowski, PhD (Age, 68)
Las Vegas, NV

Coach's Check-In

What an inspirational couple! They started an Internet marketing company when they were in their 60's and have been successful with their efforts. How have you used age as a crutch for not pursuing a new job or starting a new business?

To craft your brand strategy, here are some key questions to consider: How do you define your target market and what does the target care about?

_____
_____
_____
_____
_____
_____
_____
_____
_____
_____
_____
_____
_____
_____
_____
_____
_____

How do you currently distinguish yourself in your marketplace? If you don't know, ask two or three people who know you well, or complete the Personal Brand Assessment at Branding50.com.

_____
_____
_____
_____
_____
_____
_____

How do you make your special attributes apparent to your target market when delivering your products or services?

What are you doing currently to gain visibility for your leadership role? Or, are you the best-kept secret in your marketplace?

How are you consistent with the story you present in the marketplace?

Who are your brand builders? (These are the people who share word of your successes with others, or who help promote your brand. Usually, their generosity is spontaneous. They mention your work, or refer services to you.)

What recent successes should you share with your brand builders?

What does your brand packaging tell the marketplace about what they can expect from your services or abilities? In other words, what story does your style of dress or your marketing collateral tell others about you and your business?

In My Experience

My business, Reunions magazine, was started within months of my 50th birthday. I had been involved in social work for almost 20 years and wanted to see what was on the creative side of the mountain! Prior to starting the magazine, I had developed a PR and promotions for small businesses and non profits - the world I'd come from. I went back to my old contacts, pitched my ideas and before long, had my first clients. I kept my PR clients to help pay the expenses.

Reunions Magazine is a reader driven quarterly to aid people who are planning family, class, military and other reunions. Our ad content consisted mainly of items that were travel related to encourage reunions to meet in new and different places. I was in touch with people who had lots of contacts and who thought of me a lot, and with research, I got the magazine started. I just had to be very creative about who might read it, how to find them and how to pay for it all. (Initially, this was done with my savings.)

Visibility, Visibility, Visibility!

I wrote and sent many news releases during 1989 and 1990 when releases frequently resulted in stories in newspapers and magazines. It was a brand new idea and one not done by anyone else. As such, it got the attention of many writers and reporters. (Some of them I still hear from today!) Before the first issue of the magazine was released, I was quoted in the New York Times and the Chicago Tribune. I was in syndication and hearing from potential readers long before I had the first issue ready and in my hands! Within the first couple of years, I had appeared on all the national morning shows, as well as TV and radio across the country.

Of course, promoting the business is so very different now. There are few appearances in the media, but the web site, Facebook and even Twitter seem to get lots of attention.

I will have a second Top 10 rating in USA Today soon and a piece in Woman's World but ten years ago there were daily appearances during the summer reunion season. *My, things sure have changed!*

The Internet, and particularly our website (http://www.reunionsmag.com is a huge asset for us. We were online very early (early 1990s) and managed to establish ourselves as the place to go. We add material constantly. We have a monthly newsletter that drives traffic to the web site, particularly for information we know readers will be looking for at particular points in the planning stages. For example, close to reunion season, people are looking for ways to make sure members register, and next, what games to play and how to entertain kids at reunions. The web site is also home to podcasts and a forum for reunion planning discussion.

We have a very active Facebook site where we hold contests and promote other services such as teleconferences on planning, our onsite forum and planning workshops and seminars.

To what specifically do you attribute your success?

Success came from having an idea that no one else had **[LEADERSHIP]**. I not only had an idea that got attention but I threw myself behind the idea and worked every spare minute on it. (I still do.) I am a mighty editorial, marketing and planning department of ONE. My employees are part time but most of them have been with me since day one (20 years), and yes, they are or were my neighbors to start with. Their kids were in kindergarten when we started, and are all out of college now.

What lessons or insights would you share with others in a similar position?

Once you find something that really intrigues you, you must give yourself completely over to thinking and acting on behalf of that idea. I will never be able to retire because everything I own is tied up in Reunions Magazine. I am passionate about the product and live it day and night. It is a happy subject, and the people involved in it are very committed and generous.

What are the largest changes that have occurred as a result of your new position?

To some people, the magazine took on the taint of a travel magazine of which there are/were many and I began to be seen as a travel writer. I have been on dozens of press junkets to reunion places. I'm on Disney's A list and treated royally wherever I go. I turn down many more trips than I take and now pretty much concentrate on invites from advertisers who then get editorial for their cause.

What advice would you give or did you receive that was most helpful throughout the changes you made?

If someone is going to start a business, they must be prepared to have tunnel focus on the subject at hand and stick to it like glue. I would also recommend a very strong and committed exercise program to keep you focused and healthy. I use a daily one hour walk to think. I set an agenda before I leave and often have the problem solved by the time I return.

Edith Wagner – 72
Milwaukee, WI
Editor - Reunions Magazine

Coach's Check-In

Edith shares an example of how the application of brand strategy: Leadership, Visibility and Consistency have resulted in a sustainable business of more than 20 years.

Do you really want to leave your brand to chance? Or do you instead want to take affirmative steps to ensure that the "space" you occupy in the minds of your consumers is the positive one that you intend?

Here's what I know for sure: by age 50 you should by able to identify one or two attributes that distinguish you from others in your field. Even if you are changing careers, you certainly have talents that are leading you towards that future endeavor. Define your attributes and characteristics – how you want to be seen by others. Establish a leadership position – what you want to be known for. Gain visibility in the marketplace for that leadership role and be consistent over time.

Let's review what we have accomplished so far:

- You've identified your "then" state by writing down the highlights of your last decade.
- You've identified what you want and captured your goals – in writing – for this personal branding exercise.

- You've conducted a SWOT analysis and taken inventory of the product – you!
- You've identified your Unique Selling Proposition for each target market.
- You've written a Yellow Pages ad that will help articulate the value that you can bring to a new position or client situation.
- You are beginning to think about brand strategy, defining what makes you different and special, and making determinations about consistently communicating these attributes to others.

> ### *EXERCISE*
> With that said, what are you thinking? Write your thoughts and inspirations down now so that you can clear your head and make these thoughts work FOR you! C'mon, do a quick brain-drain…

_____
_____
_____
_____
_____
_____
_____
_____
_____
_____
_____
_____
_____
_____
_____
_____
_____

CHAPTER SIX

Applying Branding Principles to Your Product — You!

Define your Brand
Copyright, Marva Goldsmith & Associates, Inc

Leadership

Leadership is about identifying what distinguishes you from others in your field. Consider the question, "How am I a leader in my field?" You have started that journey! You have identified your goal. You have conducted a SWOT analysis. You have written your Unique Selling Proposition. You know what makes you different and special. You know why you stand out from others in your field (or at least you have placed a stake in the ground and claimed what will differentiate you from your competitors.)

In every field or endeavor imaginable there are opportunities to take a leadership role in your field of work. Identify what your leadership role will become in order to establish your niche. In Art's example, writing is his gift and passion and he has experience as a publisher. His leadership role may be as a writer who can take you from thought to print.

Visibility

Who can you think of who already does what you love to do and is successful at it? What is the difference between those people and you? Yes, you know about them, but do they know about you? That's important, too.

What have they done to become more visible? Where do you see them? Do they have websites? *Do you?* Are they associated with industry or trade organizations? *Are you?* How can you make your talent more visible with your target market; that is, in your field or within your company?

We are assuming that your skill set or quality of offerings is similar to those of the people who do what you want to do. If that is not the case, what do you need to do to get on par with your most visible competitor? You must have the courage to pursue your passion and then become known for it. If your work is not your passion, then how can you bring your passion to your work?

Consistency

Consistency is the keystone. Don't dabble in your gift, treating it like a hobby, and walk away. Ask yourself, "How can I build this into something that will grow and last?" The economic crisis certainly provides an impetus to turn your hobby into a viable business.

It's important for you to identify a leadership role and become good at delivering a consistent and quality product or service. That product or service can be delivered to clients or to your peers at work.

Branding occurs over time. That's true whether we are considering a commercial product or a person. The brand, "Marva Goldsmith, who delivers image and personal branding workshops and services," was born in 2001 and incorporated as a business on February 14, 2002. It took seven years to finally arrive at a point where my body of work was known in a niche of my desired marketplace. The community of people who know my work continues to expand as a direct result of my diligence in delivering a consistent service and a strategic emphasis on visibility. In other words, I work at it – always.

For example, a part of my branding strategy is to become more visible to human resource professionals – people who are responsible for allocating the training budgets. I've begun to accomplish this goal by speaking at Society of Human Resource Management (SHRM) conferences. In 2005, I submitted a proposal to speak at the Maryland regional conference, but that first attempt was not successful. In 2007, I submitted a proposal to speak at the SHRM regional conference in New Jersey, and that effort *was* successful! I presented a workshop on Branding YOU, Inc.

I was then invited to present the workshop at the 2008 SHRM New York conference and to expand my topic to "Branding You and HR" as the featured pre-conference presenter. That meant there were no concurrent workshops to compete against. Even better, this workshop was granted recertification credit status: participants received credit for attending.

After the New York SHRM workshop, I was invited to present in New Hampshire for their 2009 regional conference. With all of that experience and positive feedback to build upon, I also submitted a proposal to speak at the 2009 National SHRM Conference, to be held in New Orleans – the Mecca for HR professionals! Thousands attend from all over the country.

I am thrilled to report that I was accepted! Just four years after my home state's conference rejection, I spoke at the national conference. Perseverance is crucial. You should have two takeaways from this example: (1) branding happens over time, not overnight; and (2) you must remain focused and consistent –a reasonable amount of persistence doesn't hurt, either.

So, you get the idea: leadership, visibility and consistency are critical components in developing a successful personal branding strategy, whether you are over 50 or not. If you have evidence that you have a good product – that you *are* a good product – make sure the marketplace knows about it.

Brand Strategy review

My goal: Increase corporate training contracts

My strategy:

- Demonstrate **LEADERSHIP** by delivering unique "value added" personal branding workshops.
- Increase **VISIBILITY** of my *Branding You* workshop within the HR community by speaking at SHRM conferences.
- Establish track record of delivering **CONSISTENT high-quality** workshops.
- Use conference evaluations to (a) show evidence of **LEADERSHIP**; (b) obtain more speaking engagements and thus increase VISIBILITY; and (c) demonstrate **CONSISTENCY** in delivery of a good product!

Ultimately, the goal of branding is for these efforts to result in a purchase or a decision…more contracts!

Getting visibility for your leadership role can be as simple as positioning yourself as an expert by writing an article, a book, or a blog.

Art re-visited

Art has a goal and he has conducted his SWOT analysis. Now, let's create a branding strategy for Art that will help him achieve his goals. This shows the process you'll want to use for yourself.

First, let's look at Art's strengths and determine the leadership role he will play in his chosen field so we can begin to craft a niche – a focused, targetable market – for Art. Having a niche does not preclude Art from taking on business outside that narrowly identified area. A niche simply helps channel limited resources towards gaining visibility and establishing a leadership role with a particular target market. Without a niche, there is no focus. Consequently, time and resources can be wasted chasing dollars. With niche marketing, it is more likely that the dollars will come to you. That's more like it, isn't it?

Art knows what he wants. **He wants to write.** That said, what type of writer does Art want to be known as? What leadership role does he take amongst the tens of thousands of people who, like Art, have a talent for writing? What makes Art different and special? These are the coach's notes that I used to prompt Art.

Art's Brand Strategy

Leadership: I want to establish a top-tier reputation for providing excellence and professionalism across a wide spectrum of written communication. I want to be a leader by providing solid, high-quality writing that effectively and succinctly interprets, refines, and sharply focuses my client's vision – that drives his or her point home with power and authority, that maximizes the message clearly, concisely, and profoundly. I want to succeed in furthering my client's mission.

Coach's query: Art, what makes you different and special; what sets you apart from other writers and editors who want to provide excellent written communications that further their client's mission? How does your experience as a publisher enhance your role as a writer?

Art's answer:
I know the basic nuts and bolts of the publishing business, from editing through composition and manufacturing. I also know the more esoteric aspects of publishing, such as the labyrinth of copyrights, digital print-on-demand technology, CD/DVD duplication, artwork and design, and even dealing with overseas vendors and international shipping/freight forwarding companies. I also have a working understanding of postal regulations for mailing newsletters and journals (some print products will retain a raison d'être in the digital age!).

Visibility: I want to build and portray a high profile in the writing, publishing, and the broader information field as a solid, no-nonsense performer: highly efficient, intensely focused, and always on point. As a first priority, I plan to setup a website to which I can refer prospective clients, especially on-line contacts. This website will detail the expertise I possess and the services I offer and emphasize just what makes me different and special. It will highlight my value proposition.

Coach's query: What can your network of publishers provide you?

Art's answer:
I know enough people in the industry whereby a brief newsletter or blog (or a combination of the two) could be a very valuable tool. One problem is that most of my industry contacts are, or were, on the "back end" of the publishing process – typesetters, printers, digital replicators – the product "producers," in a word. However, my target audience, at least at this formative stage, consists of the "front end" creators, writers, and editors of the content to be published. Thus, I will need to work on ways to recruit the help of my primary contacts to reach out to my target audience – which could be to their benefit, too. After all, a printer's representative might be very eager to put me in touch with prospective authors or editors if he or she thought it might lead to book manufacturing contracts in the future.

Coach's query: Can you offer a bundled price? Or can you manage a project from start to finish...writing, copywriting, printing, etc. You know, "Hire Art Lizza: the No-Hassle approach to writing?"

Art's answer:
There are groups and associations devoted to writing, publishing, and self-publishing, such as Para Publishing (and many others) that I need to investigate and consider joining. I will redouble my efforts in seeking out professional and trade organizations that will help me build that high-profile visibility that I need to succeed.

I am interested in starting a "grassroots campaign" right here in my local community. I may be very surprised by the number of opportunities right in my own backyard. I believe I can get some inexpensive advertising through a host of local newspapers – the freebie papers we all get in the mail. I live in a mostly rural community with the usual sorts of local businesses that may need a writer, and I believe it is a community where it may be easy to establish a presence very quickly through a little advertising and *a lot* of word-of-mouth. Nothing fancy, no frills, no fads – just solid, reliable, and dependable performance. For example: "Need to make a case, or drive a point across with impact? Call Art."

Coach's query: Art, now that you have considered leadership and visibility, you have to manage the delivery of your message to be sure it's consistent over time.

Most people miss this element of personal branding. Branding is not a one-step, simple process, like sending out an outstanding brochure or having a great logo and tagline. Instead, effective branding is achieved and nurtured by delivering a consistent experience that target customers have come to expect and rely upon over time. And you must deliver on this promise each and every time.

Effective branding is the unwavering truth of who you are and what you represent in the marketplace – no matter the size of your market. What are the steps that you can take over time that will build your desired brand consistently?

Art's answer:
My professionalism and determination to do the job right and to get it done on time earned me a reputation for excellence, honesty, and cooperation on both the editorial and the publishing production sides. I was well respected by authors and industry insiders alike. That same dedication to excellence and to service will be critical to establish a reputation for steady-handed consistency with my future clients. These traits (brand promises) will need to be used to the fullest extent possible in all of my promotional materials, both online and in print.

In short, I see no substitute for a measured, operational standard of excellence demonstrated over time – no substitute for hard work, and certainly no quick route to achieving the consistency goal. I'll have to earn it.

"Deliverables" – a checklist of exactly what Art wants to establish (that is, his GOALS):

Leadership

- Establish a top-tier reputation for providing excellence and professionalism across a wide-spectrum of written communication
- Create communications that further a client's mission
- Capitalize on extensive publishing background and experience

Visibility

- Develop a website that emphasizes difference
- Develop a periodic newsletter for industry contacts

- Develop a blog
- Join writing, publishing, and self-publishing groups and associations
- Develop a "grassroots campaign" to become the writer of choice in the local business community

Consistency

- Deliver on time, every time
- Set a schedule for newsletter or blogging
- Identify two or three organizations to attend periodic meetings; consider a leadership role

Art has a great start on developing his goals. To make the goals more powerful, he will later develop a schedule for completing his goals.

A query for everyone: What if your goal is to find a position in the field of your choice and not to brand yourself in a new business role?

The simple process outlined in the last two chapters still applies to you. The good news is you are narrowing your scope of desired employment by defining what you want. You will find that the SWOT analysis will be invaluable in helping you to identify the job or position that best suits your needs.

You will also discover that after thoughtfully completing the SWOT analysis, you will be able to handle any interview questions about your abilities or goals, because you have now studied you – the product.

- You will be able to define what distinguishes you from others.
- You will have your leadership qualities down cold and be able to discuss them flawlessly.
- You will be able to identify opportunities to gain visibility for your leadership role.
- You will be conscious of your brand promise and will know how to consistently deliver on it.

Prep work for any field you choose

Okay, what if you're not selling a talent but instead have a talent for selling? Below is an example of a personal branding strategy to win a sales director's position.

Goal: Director of Sales
Target: Vice President of Sales

Additional tactics can be added but here are a few to get you started:

Leadership

- Distinguish yourself in the top tier of sales producers within your organization or industry.

Visibility

- Volunteer to provide sales training for new recruits or under-performers within the organization.
- Volunteer to create a sales "training tips" manual.
- Participate in formal management training programs and/or seminars. Consistency
- Continue to deliver on top-tier performance numbers.
- Identify industry organizations that use your product and get active; participate in meetings, network, and/or take on a leadership position.

CHAPTER SEVEN

Passion and Branding

Copyright, Marva Goldsmith & Associates, Inc

A passion for your brand – and turning your passion into a brand

In the first section of this book, I showed you the process of creating a brand strategy. In this next section, we will drill down to mine your core interests.

Coach's Nudge:

If you are having trouble creating a brand strategy for yourself, take five minutes to clear your mind. Free your thoughts of daily stresses and mortgage payments and ask yourself, "What in life gives me the greatest pleasure?" Notice I didn't say anything about ways to earn money; don't filter your answer by factoring in possible sources of income. Just identify that one thing that makes you smile every single time you do it.

For me, this has always been shopping (and thus, an electrical engineer becomes an image consultant). For some, as with Art, it may be writing. For others, maybe it's painting, woodworking, talking to people, working with numbers, building things…you get the idea.

Now imagine combining your gifts with your passion. For example, if painting is your gift and nature is your passion, become known for creating masterpieces of landscaped beauty, or painting a series on endangered species.

In My Experience...

Three years ago, I was happy, successful and working in a different industry. My associate and long time friend, Ken Pomerance, walked into my office and asked me what I thought about creating a Facebook-like social network for the 12 Step recovery community. I sat there for a second and yelled YES, of course, let's do it! We haven't looked back since – that was April 26, 2007.

I had been President of Extreme Promotions and Events, Inc. I was ready for something more and different; something that helps people every day. In The Rooms.com is an online social network for those in recovery, seeking help and their families and friends.

When I made the decision to join Ken and create In The Rooms, my life made a significant change spiritually. I wake up every day feeling whole, knowing I am doing something that is good for the global recovering community and humanity at large. I have truly found what drives me. It is my passion for helping others and standing up for what I believe in. I have realized now that my happiness and fulfillment is an inside job and comes from opening my heart and giving back to others unconditionally. I'm loving every minute of it!

What advice would you give or did you receive that was most helpful throughout the changes you made?

Identify an idea you are passionate about, then start out small and build on the idea. Know that every door that closes, another will open. And learn from others. Before we even started the site, my co-founder, Ken

Pomerance, and I flew out to California to learn from the best in social networking. The most important advice is to execute.

What were the first steps you took once you knew a change was coming?

For Ken and I, we knew that everything was about getting the In The Rooms site launched. So we took the following steps to entrepreneurial success:

We chose a great name for a recovery site, In The Rooms. In The Rooms (www.intherooms.com) is a term used in all 12 step fellowships (AA, NA, GA, OA, etc.) that helps maintain anonymity. For example, instead of saying to someone at a party, "Didn't I see you at an AA or NA meeting," I would say "Don't I know you from In The Rooms?"

We developed our vision on a yellow legal pad which quickly transcended onto the back of one of my daughter's science boards. Since we both have been in long term recovery for over a quarter of a century, we knew what we would want in a social network for the global recovery community.

In the beginning, In The Rooms world headquarters was my house. We began assembling a team with our limited budget, financed by me, and hired a part time developer and web designer to build a platform. Before we began our fundraising we set out to California to meet with some social networking gurus to listen and learn.

Ken and I put together a PowerPoint presentation that we could take with us on our quest for investors. We may have used the PowerPoint once before we realized it was boring. We decided to just explain our vision and let our honesty and passion speak for itself. It worked. The first ten people we presented our business plan to wrote us a check and we were on our way to make our dream become a reality.

What strategies did you employ to find a new position, or find customers for your new business?

Since our business is a social network, all of our efforts were very viral. Once the site had launched, Ken and I relied on our recovery community network and then word seemed to spread like wildfire.

In The Rooms has been growing ever since. Within 18 months of our launch on October 6, 2008, In The Rooms has become the number one trafficked recovery based social network in the world with more than 90,000 members in over 50 countries representing over 240,000 years of recovery. In The Rooms currently has 18 different 12-Step fellowships represented and there is more to come. We feature a vast speakers tape library, daily meditations, a worldwide meeting list for AA, NA, GA and OA, blogs, forums, discussions, four ways to communicate including private and instant messaging, comments, and status updates. In The Rooms has over 1200 affinity groups to choose from or you can start a group of your own that fits your needs.

What lessons or insights would you share with others in a similar position?

There are a lot of great ideas however it's the execution of the idea that is most important. It takes vision, time, dedication, focus and perseverance to execute any idea correctly.

How is your new job different from what you have done in the past, if at all?

In the past, I also loved what I did to make a living. Now I love what I do and it's driven by my passion to put a positive face on recovery and help others. Together, we will make the world a better place to live.

Ron Tannebaum
Fort Lauderdale, Florida.
Age: 59

WORKSHEET:

Create Your Brand Strategy
Using the answers to the questions posed in Chapter Five, define the following essential elements. (I told you we would use that information later.)

LEADERSHIP: How are you distinguishing yourself in your marketplace?

_____
_____
_____
_____
_____
_____
_____
_____
_____
_____

VISIBILITY: What are you doing to gain visibility for yourself in your leadership role?

CONSISTENCY: In what ways do you need to be consistent with the story you are presenting in the marketplace?

CHAPTER EIGHT

Sue's Story

Leap of Faith

Copyright, Marva Goldsmith & Associates, Inc

Let's reinforce the lessons by example. Meet Sue Thompson.

Then: Turning 40

At the end of 1996, the year I turned 40, I completed a Master of Clinical Psychology Degree at Antioch University in Los Angeles. However, by the time I graduated and completed my internship, I'd discovered that providing therapy was not my thing after all.

I was disappointed by this discovery but *not* with the degree, although I wasn't sure how to use it. I was sick of Los Angeles and wanted a change of seasons, a change of pace, and a change of life. I found a job as the office manager for a small company in Delaware. My husband was waiting for a buy-out from a savings and loan that was changing hands so we lived apart for a while, catching time together every couple of months when we traveled for business. We were childless, by choice, making this possible.

I took on more responsibilities at work, received training, and did whatever I knew I could do. As a middle manager I was in the perfect spot: I didn't have to participate in the big, strategic decisions a vice president would have to, but I executed orders well and liked being in command of those I managed.

In my late 40s, I got involved in some management initiatives and training that reignited my love of psychology, temperament studies, and personality development. And I rediscovered a talent I'd pushed to the back burner for a long time – public speaking. For years, colleagues in professional organizations had asked me to share my ideas at staff meetings and chapter events, and it finally became clear to me that I spoke with authority and that people perceived me to be an expert.

Coach's Tip:

Other people can help you identify your strengths. Are you listening to them?

I took some motivational courses in public speaking and started making contacts, one of which resulted in my writing and publishing *The Prodigal Brother: Making Peace with Your Parents, Your Past, and the Wayward One in Your Family*, which was published by Tyndale House in June 2005 – the year before my 50th birthday.

www.amazon.com/Prodigal-Brother-Making-Parents-Wayward/dp/1589972597

Turning 50 – and rekindling my real passion

I was doing more speaking and gradually made that my focus. I went to seminars on how to build a consulting business, participated in teleseminars on various related topics, and read about others who had followed their leadings to do things that turned out to be timely and successful. My job as a facility manager was becoming less and less important to me, but my connection to my professional organization opened other doors. I spoke several times at the annual convention, presented at my local chapter, and wrote an article for the association's monthly journal.

When I recognized how very possible it was to do what made my heart sing, to turn the activities that excited and energized me into a business, I followed the leading. I started with creating some great promotional materials, thanks to my husband, and taking the other needed steps to start a business.

Coach's Note

Sue discovered a passion that was linked to her strength – public speaking – and then took action. Note that she also engaged in retooling.

Ministry and me

When I was much younger, I was a guest speaker in churches. I did this for a number of years and, in fact, met my husband during one of my long stays in a town where I had ministered. I'm not an evangelist; I'm more of a teacher, which is very common in the church circles where I held Bible-centered seminars and conferences.

I incorporated my ministry as People Set Free Ministries. Over those years, I occasionally spoke at women's retreats or church meetings. In 2005, when I was 49, a Christian publishing house released my book, *The Prodigal Brother*. To promote the book, I did numerous radio interviews throughout the country, wrote articles for magazines, and even participated in a television program that featured the book. My husband created a stunning multimedia CD that included me reading an excerpt of the book and telling of my ministry, and I sent it to 300 churches throughout the United States and Canada.

I thought the book was going to throw the doors wide open for me. I thought the ministry would explode with requests for speaking engagements and writings, but I did not receive one single request for my services. Not one! **NOT ONE.**

Can I explain to you how strange that was? I'd worked with other church speakers who had poorly designed websites, had not written a book, and who had mediocre or even poor presentation skills. Yet they had steady engagements and some even managed to support themselves with their ministry work. By contrast, I had this marvelous gift of having had a book published by a reputable house, and I had sent out a truly outstanding piece of promotional material to what was essentially my target market – and absolutely nothing happened. It was so odd and unexpected that I could not get upset about it. I just pondered the meaning. And then I had a dream.

In the dream, my husband married someone else while he was still married to me. (As dreams usually go, this made perfect sense. You know how weird they can be!) His other wife had a terminal illness, and my husband felt it was important that he be married to her for the remainder of her life. I accepted that, even though I was very sad. I love my husband deeply and can't imagine life without him, but in the dream he didn't belong to just me anymore. He might again someday, I told myself, but not now; I had to let him go.

I awoke with a profound sadness that clung to me for days. I ruminated upon that dream, rolling over the possible interpretations. I knew the dream meant something and I wanted to benefit from its wisdom. I talked to my pastor about it, and I told him I thought it might mean that I was supposed to put the ministry aside completely for now. At a time when the opportunities for my ministry should be popping up like daisies, my efforts were producing nothing, and it was time to let it go. Maybe the opportunity will return to me someday, I told him, but it's not mine right now.

What I was getting instead, I explained to my pastor, was requests for speaking engagements, and I had ideas that I wanted to pursue. I thought I could make a real go of the business, in ways I couldn't explain, I said, and thought it might be my true calling. I even had a name for it: "Set Free Life Seminars." I am all about the lessons of life and how they can set us free if we receive them in the right way. I speak with an authority that makes people want to listen to me. I have a joy that spills over and is invigorating and entertaining. I think this is what God wants me to do, I told my pastor.

He listened and helped confirm that I was traveling in the right direction. I established Set Free Life Seminars, LLC. I started compiling my ideas. I took baby steps, feeling my way carefully but determined to move forward.

A secular mission: weight reduction and control

To make my leap forward, I had to let go of some things that were important to me. I had put a lot of work into my ministry. My job was no longer fulfilling – and I was in the throes of menopause.

My worst menopause symptoms were hot flashes and a metabolism that dropped like a stone. It had never been great; I'd had a weight problem all of my life. I remember my mother lamenting over how fat I was when I was only eight years old. I weighed 150 pounds when I was in junior high school. In high school, I was the "fat girl" who never had a boyfriend. In all of my adult years, the least I ever weighed was around 160, and that was a brief and shining moment. I had done the Cambridge Diet (the original liquid diet), the Cabbage Soup Diet, and most recently, the Atkins Diet. Atkins was great for me. My body actually does its best on a low-carb diet and I love all of the food I can eat on that plan. Earlier, I'd lost 40 pounds, but had gained back 20 over the next couple of years.

I started following Atkins again, religiously, when I set up "Set Free Life Seminars," but this time, even Atkins stopped working, and my weight shot up to well above 200 pounds. I decided it was now or never. I could not stand in front of people with so much excess weight and talk about how great life could be. I made an initial goal of losing 20 pounds and followed the Weight Watcher's Points system like my life depended upon it. I had been exercising off and on, but I stepped it up and made sure I did some exercise every day.

I lost 21 pounds during the 10-week meeting cycle, and I was thrilled. I'm not one to need cheerleading when it comes to personal commitments so I didn't sign up for the next round of meetings, but I kept up the program. It had not been difficult, and I thought I'd just keep it up as long as I could. My husband, the cook in our relationship, had gotten used to my needs and accommodated me with fantastic salads (which he also enjoyed!) and delicious preparations of chicken, fish and vegetables. I had everything I needed for success, so I thought, "Why not stick with it?"

A few months passed and another 20 pounds came off. I wasn't losing quickly – that's never happened for me. My body is as resistant to weight loss as they come but I was losing consistently and I wasn't constantly hungry.

My new business was growing. I was getting conference speaking engagements, including some for a new lecture that I was very excited about: "Acting Like a Leader in a Hostile Work Environment." I actually *had* learned something during my dark night of the Big Project and the ensuing difficulties with the company president, and I outlined the principles that had gotten me through. The presentation was an enormous success. People stood in line to talk with me, to cry on my shoulder as they told me of their own severe situations, and to tell me it was the best seminar of the conference. My evaluations were fantastic. I began to entertain the thought of writing a book on the subject and even started on a few chapters. It had become my next important thing, and I began looking for a book agent or an acquisitions editor.

These successes were accompanied by personal victories. More months went by, and more pounds came off. Now I was into an exercise routine that had me looking fit and feeling healthy. People were commenting on my weight loss every day. I had to buy new clothes and, oh my! I don't know why it was easy for me this time. This doesn't mean I didn't have days when I blew it or that I wasn't tempted at all.

The truth was, somewhere along the line food had ceased to be a huge issue for me. I didn't fight urges anymore; food was no longer my most important comforter. I didn't see my body as an enemy anymore, either. I had acknowledged early on that if I was going to lose, the weight was going to come off slowly because that's the way my body responds. I decided not to let it derail me, but to just stick with it as long as I could tolerate the deprivation. It turned out I didn't feel deprived at all. My husband's great cooking certainly had something to do with that!

It took me from March 2007 to roughly the time of my birthday in July of 2008 – that's 15 or 16 months – to lose 75 pounds. Along the way I had to dedicate myself to a sincere lifestyle change, exercising *every single day*. I've done this occasionally throughout my life and have never maintained the effort, but now that I have decided this is the way it's going to be, I can honestly say that when I am running, or working on my Total Gym, or doing Pilates, *I feel young!* I feel in control. I feel like my whole life is ahead of me and, of course, it is. We are living in a day and age when it is becoming more and more possible to live to 100 years old and still be in good health, if we make wise choices.

I still can't believe I've lost so much weight! I am in the 130s, way below the lowest weight I'd ever seen previously in my adult life. I probably last weighed what I do now when I was 12 years old. I wear a size 2! It feels like a release. It feels like losing the weight is a symbol of being set free. I am a living symbol.

I believe my new feelings about my body and my abilities are a leap into a new place. People talk a lot about "going to the next level," whatever they think that means, but they are terrified of the actual leap. I don't think we get to the next level by just walking up a couple of stairs; it takes a true act of faith to jump out into the darkness and reach for that which is ahead. So many get to the threshold and – no matter how ready they are, or how much talent and desire they have – they stop at that threshold and start telling themselves why they should *not* make the leap, at least not yet. Pretty soon they've backed away, losing the energy needed to propel them to the place that is waiting for them, ready for them – the place of expansion. I do not want to be 75 years old, or 85 – or even 60 – saying to myself, "I should have jumped. I wish I'd just throw caution to the wind. I should have done it."

> "Sometimes you just have to take the leap,
> and grow your wings on the way down."
> – African proverb

Sue's personal inventory

Relationship builder, seer (ability to identify talent and abilities in people), encourager, mystic with a ridiculous optimism about what is possible.

Sue's goal

I want to have a successful business that makes me available to people who desire to move forward and who need someone to show them *their* way – not a canned or off-the-shelf way. I want to speak, write, and instruct. I want people to feel I gave them something they truly needed, even if they did not realize they needed it when they started their journey. I want to change lives.

I want to make enough money in my business that I don't need to worry about whether or not I can actually make enough money.

Sue's SWOT

STRENGTHS:

- Relationship builder
- Ability to identify talent and match people to assignments (understanding their strengths)
- Ridiculous demand for excellence. I subscribe to the mantra of Louis XIV, who made France synonymous with style and good taste: *Stick to the high end and forget the low. Never underestimate the importance of décor and ambiance.*[1] Do it beautifully and do it well. Proofread, proofread, and proofread. Write intelligently. Put thought and care into projects. Execute with style. Good design is good marketing
- Ease in front of groups
- Quick decision maker
- Love of learning and teaching
- Deep desire to see lives changed

WEAKNESSES:

- I can get very scared. I can second-guess myself ruthlessly.
- I have to fight against a fear of not having what I need to move forward (a particular degree, certain experiences, or a way of thinking).
- I am judgmental and critical. I'm impatient with people who don't share my standards for excellence. Sometimes I write them off. I do not like this about myself. I pray that I am successful at keeping it private, as I have no desire to offend anyone.
- I don't discipline myself in scheduling and meeting goals. I'm not always sure this is necessary, but if it is, I'm not good at it.

OPPORTUNITIES:

- I'm unafraid to go after knowledge I need. As always, I'll take every class, pursue new avenues, find the people who can offer what I'm missing, and storm heaven to fill in my gaps. I'm doing it now by

---
[1] Joan DeJean, *The Essence of Style: How the French Invented High Fashion, Fine Food, Chic Cafes, Style, Sophistication, and Glamour.* New York: Free Press, 2005.

pursuing high-end management consulting instruction because I believe I need to play with the big boys and girls.
- I believe the book I'm writing can be a bestseller. I believe it will truly help people and they will buy it because they are desperate for answers.
- I believe people are concerned about the importance of character and the lack of it in our society. This creates tremendous opportunities for me to be the character expert.

THREATS:

- Finances can constrain. It often takes money to make money, but I am only willing to increase my credit limit with MasterCard or Visa by so much. Excellence costs money. The training I need costs money. I need more money.
- Personal energy: I have to make sure I rest after completing big things. When I become depleted, I get angry and cranky and full of despair and self-doubt. This is when I always know I need a nap or a vacation, but the desire to push forward and skip those times of replenishment is huge. It's a constant struggle.

A conversation between Sue and Marva

Coach: A couple of questions are still hanging out there for me. What is your position on the *Prodigal Son* book and your initial strategy to engage your target audience around that work?

    Sue: When I had that dream, I felt it was a message for me to put that part of my life aside for now and go for the "secular" pursuit of my business. The book was heavily promoted for a good six months. Then I sent my mailing. I sold the book whenever I spoke in churches or at women's retreats. It just seemed to come to a slow stop. I finally came to believe that book was supposed to be written for – someone, maybe a few people? I don't know – who truly needed it.

    Based on the parable Jesus told of the prodigal son, who demanded his inheritance from his father and then ran off and squandered it in wild living, the book is about the struggles of growing up. My parents devoted their entire lives to rescuing my alcoholic, drug-addicted brother, while I stood on the sidelines watching my family self-destruct. In the parable, the prodigal son comes home and the father, overjoyed, throws a huge party. His older son, frustrated and filled with resentment, tells him, "I stayed with you all these years and you never threw a party for me!" I saw myself as that older son, who simply needed acknowledgment that in the middle of all the chaos, he mattered.

I think this project will come back later for an "unveiling." It's in the background now.

Coach: What was the product or service that was being offered to the churches? Are you totally abandoning this product/strategy? Is there a different target? Was there additional work done after the 300 church mailings? What was the outcome? Did you talk with the churches where you had conducted the seminars regarding the book and service offerings? What was their reason for not responding to your offer?

Sue: I didn't follow up. I was going to sit down and start making calls, but I seized up. I didn't know how to be comfortable promoting myself in that manner. I was still burned out from the job disaster. Then I gave that talk at the business conference and it started to turn my head toward the new speaking niche.

I'm still invited by churches as a guest speaker on various topics. I haven't abandoned it. I still receive calls for women's retreats and I'll do a Sunday morning service somewhere or a Wednesday night. Sometimes a three-night meeting on, say, how to know your gifts. Perhaps the activity of the ministry will come back to me again instead of merely being a side activity.

Coach: I am interested in seeing you create a branding strategy around the book since you have made this investment of time and resources, and the book has received high ratings. It just seems that there is more to be done with the book.

Sue: I prefer to look at my current market. Interestingly, though, my husband wants me to create a strategy around the book. He's already started on a website just for the book – and now you're saying this, too. Maybe it's something I should pay attention to.

In My Experience...

In 2002, I had the desire for a change and to use my creative talents more. I had a small part time business in the past that allowed me to be creative and it had done well. I also had experience working in retail merchandising and display for Williams-Sonoma, Pottery Barn, Hold Everything and The Original Christmas Store. Still, I wasn't sure that I was ready to give up the security of my full time profession.

I had been working as a Licensed Radiology Tech and Certified Medical Assistant for 12 years. My leaving meant a big change for everyone. The prospect of having to train and adjust to a new employee was going to be stressful for everyone. There was some resentment but there was also happiness for me. After that many years in a practice we had become close. It was a difficult decision to make because I enjoyed my work and knew I would miss it. It was exciting and a little scary, but once I made the decision I knew it was the right one. I've never regretted it. My employer took the office to lunch at an upscale restaurant for my going away party and gave me a very generous gift certificate to my favorite clothing boutique so I could start off my new career in style.

I did research on professional organizations for interior redesign and read everything I could find on the subject I took an intensive training and certification course in interior redesign and real estate staging offered by the organization I felt offered the best support to its members, the Interior Redesign Industry Specialists (IRIS). I also read as much as I could about best business practices for small businesses. I checked out insurance plans, required business licenses, computer programs, needed equipment and wrote a business plan.

I joined IRIS and became listed on their online national directory; told everyone I knew that I had started my new business and asked them to tell all of their friends. I was soon asked to donate gift certificates for my services to fundraisers for schools and organizations. I introduced myself to kindred spirit businesses and offered to do presentations for their customers. For groups and organizations, I did presentations at their meetings that tied redesign and decorating into their interests and participated in charity events where I could use my talents to help their efforts. I checked out networking groups; participated in a Business and Design Show House and a regional Home Show; took out business ads in local directories and newspapers; and mailed out fliers and brochures.

How did people/recruiters/businesses learn about you?

I raised awareness of my business through the following: word of mouth from clients, presentations, my web site (www.FaulknerHouse.com) and newsletter, a listing in the Redesigner's Notebook and other online directories, profiles on Linkedin and Active Rain, articles where I have been featured or quoted and press releases about awards and contests I have won have raised awareness of my business.

What lessons or insights would you share with others in a similar position?

- Do your homework. Learn everything you can about your new career and about how to conduct a business.
- Do follow through on every promise and every task
- Do a reality check-are you willing to put in the amount of time it will take to create the foundation of your business and keep it running? If business is slow to take off, will you lose interest?
- Do you have the support of those whose opinions you value? If you don't, will you be able to go on?
- Do you have the abilities and talents required? Are you willing to take additional courses to keep up with current trends or best business practices?
- Don't go into a new career or business as a whim.
- Do something you love and have always wanted to do.
- Don't underestimate the amount of time it will take on a day to day basis.

- Don't forget to budget your time. A business can take over your life, or it will die if you don't tend to it on a regular basis.
- Don't undervalue your services or your time.

If you hit a bump in the road, don't allow it to paralyze you instead use the obstacle to propel you into action.

Three years after forming my business, I didn't hit a bump, I hit a brick wall. A freak accident left me with a complicated spinal fracture and an uncertain future. My first decision was to contact current clients to explain what had happened. I was overwhelmed by the understanding and support I received. Most \of my clients patiently waited for me to recover so that I could work on their projects. I was touched by their loyalty and I have tried to repay this kindness many times over the years.

What are the largest changes that have occurred as a result of your new position?

I continue to be amazed by the opportunities presented to me as my business has grown. I give presentations about design and decorating and was asked to be a speaker at a national home show three years ago. I ended up doing a presentation following that of a well- known HGTV celebrity –this from a woman who dreaded every moment of her Speech 101 course in college. Two years later, I was invited to be a speaker at a women's retreat in West Virginia by the event's organizer who had seen my presentation at the home show.

I formed a group of IRIS redesigners in the area five years ago for the purpose of networking. It became the IRIS National Capital Area Chapter last year and received national recognition for its makeovers of three apartments for a local family homeless shelter. Articles about the project appeared in the Washington Post, Philanthropy Today and other publications – even The Standard, China's only English business newspaper! As the first president of the new chapter, I was honored to accept the Community Partner Award presented by Shelter House for our groups' efforts.

We were also presented with an official copy of the United States Congressional Record for June 9, 2009, in which

Congressman Gerald R. Connolly of Virginia recognized "Shelter House.org and in particular the contributions its volunteers make in service to our community" and named the Interior Redesign Industry Specialists as the Community Partner Award winners for the Patrick Henry Shelter Project.

What advice would you give or did you receive that was most helpful throughout the changes you made?

Follow your dream but do it with your eyes wide open and your feet firmly on the ground. Face your fears. If you have made all the proper preparations and are willing to take on the challenges of creating and running your own business, take that leap and give it your all. You never know how you may grow or where your business will take you.

I have grown personally and professionally from taking that leap of faith in starting a new business. It has been an adventure that no business plan would ever have anticipated or predicted.

Pamela Faulkner
Herndon/Oak Hill, VA
Age: 59

CHAPTER NINE

The Retreat

Copyright, Marva Goldsmith & Associates, Inc

Crossroads at the Crossings: September

As I mentioned at the beginning of the book, when I first considered what I would do for my 50th birthday, one idea was to treat myself to a spa retreat. I know it's just September and my birthday is not until December but I've decided to enjoy a significant event every month! **If not NOW, when?**

So here I am at the Crossings in Austin, Texas. A time-out is warranted.

I'm here because I found a workshop that is so on-point that if I didn't know better, I'd say someone ripped my brain open, read my thoughts, and designed it just for me. **It's for women in transition.**

I enter the gates of the Crossings. The adventure begins as I zigzag along the winding roads that lead to the reception house, sanctuary, spa and guesthouses. I pass robed guests who appear to be in some sort of transcendental state, apparently having just left the spa. (Wow, can't wait for my treatment!) I venture out to the deck where I see others with nametags and recognize them as part of my group. Two lovely young women, Sara and Kathy, invite me to their table and we exchange pleasantries and pearls of wisdom. My 20 or so fellow participants come primarily from the Austin and Houston areas plus one from Michigan, one from Phoenix and two from California; their ages range from 30 to 71, including a host of other mid-century divas.

With anticipation for tomorrow's activities, I retreat to my room for the night. It is nestled a short distance back, among beautiful shrubs, driftwood, cacti, and aloe vera plants meticulously arranged along the walking paths. I walk briskly as the scenery seems ripe for a coyote or two to be hidden in the terrain, crouching and ready to strike!

The guest rooms are very nice, but spartan; there is no TV or Internet in my room. **Wait a minute!** *No Internet??* What the heck am I going to do for an outside connection with the rest of the world? Okay, relax...I can do this. There's Internet and TV in the public spaces, so I just have to make it until morning. I take a deep breath. *Maybe I really do need a time-out.* I did not leave my Black(*crack*)Berry® or my laptop at home. In truth, that would *not* have been a peaceful experience – not for me.

My room has a Zen-like setting. I turn on the sleep machine that's situated next to my bed, tuning it to a classical music station (instead of the crickets or ocean sounds). It is lovely. As I type into my Internet-less laptop, I feel as if I'm playing along with the orchestra – the keyboard as my instrument, words are my notes – in harmony with the sounds I am hearing. I fall asleep listening to a beautiful symphony.

This retreat center is known for healthy exercise and food: yoga, meditation, massage, bean sprouts – that whole transcendental experience. I rise with the sun, (which is about 6:30 a.m. here), and reflect on life.

What is my intention for this weekend?

I intend to have a retreat experience that is rich and inspiring, with lasting effects. I hope to gain an insight or two that will lead me toward more fulfillment in my life. I plan to explore, to seek knowledge, **to stop wrestling with things I cannot control.**

First insights: Stop complaining about the things I can control and get into action; be happy in nothingness, recognizing that it alone is pure potential, and listen to the sound of silence.

What's clear is that I am grateful for my life. I know what I have is abundant and good and enough in *this* moment.

> "(A) rich person is not one who has the most, but is one who needs the least."
> – William Kroll, An Interview with God

I have clarity of thought, creative spirit, and the fortitude to continue to listen; to give; and to receive bountiful blessings.

From this space in time, I look back on a half-century of living and acknowledge that it has been good and I am well. Perfect? No; but, all is well.

In this space, I am open to new possibilities and in this **moment** I will create new possibilities. I'm able to move forward and accept that yesterday was just that – *yesterday*. And, that all my yesterdays are complete.

Given that I am turning 50, I thought this retreat would be all about me figuring out how to **BE** in this next phase in life and that it would offer a relaxing time to write this book.

The retreat, however, proves to be much more than that for me; it focuses on **self-care.** I guess that is how I want to BE in this next phase of life anyway: fully engaged while I ensure that I am taking care of *me* in a very special and complete way.

Keys to good health and well-being

Self-care: Taking care of one's self. *"Oh, I already do that,"* you might say. Some people do, but what I discovered is that I am not one of those people.

Oh, I buy myself the pretty trinkets, treat myself to good meals, indulge in a quarterly housecleaning, and great trips. But, then there are the fundamental missteps: I allowed myself to gain 20 pounds over the past five years; I exercise only once a week; I am my worst critic; I take on *way* too much, so I work 12 to 16 hours a day – *almost every day*. I don't connect with friends and family often enough. (Who am I kidding – there's no time.) *This does not constitute "taking care of me."* The only self-care that I provide consistently is mental self-care through continuous learning. *Does any of this sound familiar? How are you* taking care of yourself?

The retreat workshop focused on four key facets of a quality life: physical, mental, spiritual, and emotional development. As we approach or experience our Golden Age, there will be challenges and changes to encounter in each of these realms.

Here's what we are told:

PHYSICAL: Physical self-care is essential. Physical changes are apparent, but we can take steps now to nourish our bodies through diet, exercise, and rest.

While at the Crossings, I met other dynamic divas whose physical self-care has honored their bodies. Their bodies are toned. They are runners and marathoners; they have exercise routines and are conscious of what they eat.

EMOTIONAL: Emotional self-care involves being kind to ourselves, watching our internal "self-talk" and our actions. Emotional self-care acknowledges the need for support, either through friends and family or through more formal support systems (e.g., therapists, coaches, career counselors, support groups, and yes, **image consultants**). I am so guilty of giving in to "being old" and actually speaking those words! Well, not anymore. **50 IS NOT OLD!** *(That felt good!)*

SPIRITUAL: Spiritual self-care may come through meditation, prayer, or communing with nature. You find guidance, direction, and support. Some find spiritual self-care by engaging in creative endeavors: playing music, drawing, writing, singing, or dancing. I would also list massage in this area, as the massage that I received at the Crossings was truly a spiritual experience.

MENTAL: Mental self-care means stimulating the mind, whether through books, workshops, course work, or movies; we must stay tuned-up for the journey.

Are you taking good care of yourself? Are you in need of self-care? Are you creating balance in your life?

To find out more, visit reneetrudeau.com, or sign up for her Self-Renewal Retreats at the Crossings. *(Tell them Marva sent you.)*

The workshops offered at my September birthday retreat taught me that I must take time out, be in the present, give myself a break, and most importantly, create more balance in my life. I must learn to nurture my body and spirit, **especially in my 50s.**

I commit to establish new habits in my life, in each of these four key facets – starting NOW!

And you can, too!

So, what's the connection between self-care and personal branding?

No matter what you want to do, or how you want to be known, success requires operating at full throttle – looking good and feeling good. Even more importantly, in this new and rapidly changing market economy we must create an environment, both internal and external, that is conducive to learning, thriving, and adapting. Focusing on and refining your brand identity will empower you in this process. And let's face it, the more you take care of yourself – get the rest you need, eat the foods that fuel the body, and exercise your body and your brain – the younger you look!

> *EXERCISE*
> Fill out the following chart:

- In the left column, identify your current level of self-care in each of the key areas.
- In the right column, describe in specific detail the new habits you will implement to better care for the brand you are launching.

Current State of Self-Care	New Empowering Habits
Mental	
Spiritual	
Emotional	
Physical	

Let's review what you have accomplished thus far:

- **You've identified your THEN state,** describing the highlights of your last decade.
- **You've identified your GOAL;** what you want to achieve in this personal branding exercise.
- **You've conducted a SWOT analysis** and taken inventory of the internal and external strengths and weaknesses of the product, YOU. You have also identified external opportunities and threats that can be a help or a hindrance in reaching your goal.
- **You've identified your Unique Selling Proposition** for each target market.
- **You've written a Yellow Pages ad** that will help articulate the value that you can bring to a new position or client situation.
- **You've developed a BRAND strategy,** identifying how to strategically reach your goals: leadership, visibility, & consistency.
- **You've created a plan for SELF-CARE,** to nurture your mental, spiritual, emotional and physical self, in order to maximize your delivery.

Coach's Tip:

This is a good time to check in with a business associate – someone you trust. You may consider a friend or family member, but I suggest you first consult with someone who can give you objective feedback within the context of your profession. Family and friends may root for you to stay "rooted" right where you are.

In My Experience...

I had moved to Los Angeles in 1994 when I heard that Hollywood needed more blondes. As a comic you only work about 30 minutes a day, so I began volunteering at a shelter for sexually abused teens. It changed my life. It woke up the healer in me and prompted me to pursue a doctorate in psychology and to specialize in the prevention and healing of child sexual abuse. If you had told me back then that I would become a psychotherapist, I would have suggested you get a psych evaluation! But now I see that "The road from comedy to mental health is very short, indeed."

Most people were THRILLED I left entertainment...and very proud that I attained a doctoral degree and became a professional. I now treat many creative artists in Hollywood.

What were the first steps you took once you knew a change was coming?

I took care of my health and fitness first and foremost, and surrounded myself with positive, supportive people. I got a game plan and stayed very disciplined and looked forward toward my goals, not backward with any regrets.

I was in school for 5 years and had great teachers and counselors there who guided me every step of the way. I just trusted them and did everything they told me to do. I understand that part of being a good leader is first being a good follower: listening to those ahead of me and just "waxing on and waxing off."

I used all my transferrable skills from comedy, which really is sales and marketing if you think about it. Comics sell themselves. I used my humor, heart, creativity, and again, followed advice of those who were already doing it. I joined networking organizations and did public speaking, wrote articles, got a kick-ass website, cable TV ads, print, cold calls, etc.

If social media has been a part of your strategy, please tell us how your success was affected by its use?

It is, but not dependently so. My website is one of my most powerful tools as is my book (*YOU-TURN: CHANGING DIRECTION IN MIDLIFE*).

What lessons or insights would you share with others in a similar position?

Follow your heart and go with your gut. Expect setbacks and obstacles, and take the lessons from them and let the pain go. Make sure you respect your job and field. Would you think highly of it if you were not in it?

What are the largest changes that have occurred as a result of your new position?

I have a completely new life. I am a professional. I quadrupled my salary in the first year. I lost my negativity and depression and cynicism. I quit smoking cigarettes. I found peace of mind. I like myself now.

What advice would you give or did you receive that was most helpful throughout the changes you made?

No advice, but I offer one of my favorite quotes that really helped me deal with the "OMG, am I too old to do this?" fears: "How old would you be if you didn't know how old you were?" (Coach's note: I'll add one to this... "You'll be the same age in 5 years with the degree or without the degree.")

Is there anything else that you want to share with others or words of wisdom?

Change is inevitable: either affect it or accept it. Wisdom comes from failure.

Dr. Nancy B. Irwin
Los Angeles, CA
Age 54

Peer review

Discuss your branding strategy with someone whose assessment will be completely objective and based on just the information provided — not someone who may be predisposed to an emotional or judgmental response to your decisions.

Family members may feel you're "throwing away" what Landmark Education terms your "probable-almost-certain-future." This is based on the presupposition that tomorrow will simply be a continuation of today and yesterday because you will not change. Those who are threatened by your desire to change — and those who are emotionally invested in the status quo — may not be the best people to help you sever the roots that confine you to your past patterns, enabling you to grow.

This does not suggest that all that has been accomplished should be diminished. Give yourself permission to explore passions that may be totally opposite to what you have done in the past. Remember, the *author* is an electrical engineer turned image consultant.

If you are reading this book as a part of a book club, partner with someone (or two) in the club to obtain this feedback. You may want to check back with this person (or persons) after you have completed this action guide.

Family Matters

When you have completed the ACTIONS, which means you will have completed your NOW state and developed an action plan (Chapters Eleven and Twelve), you may *then* want to bring in your loved ones. Discuss your plan and get their input and support. Make sense?

Connect with Me

How are you doing? This may be a great time for you to check in with me or another coach. Take this moment to visit my blog at Branding50.com. Send a question, or make a comment. I would love to hear how you are progressing with this work. **Note: If you are reading this book in the year 2018, do not visit my blog – I'm now retired!**

CHECK IN

What have you learned about yourself?

_____
_____
_____
_____
_____
_____
_____

What do you think about your possibilities?

CHAPTER TEN

Lessons from Dolly: Your Package

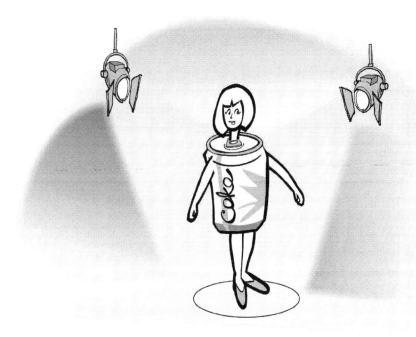

" Package Your Brand "
Copyright, Marva Goldsmith & Associates, Inc

What we can learn about image from DOLLY?

Beautiful and vivacious, she is known for her curvaceous body and her beautiful voice. I recently watched the icon on *The Tonight Show*. As she sat talking with Jay Leno, I was surprised – as I am sure other viewers were – to hear that she was 62 years old. **Wow! She looked great!**

That is, until she stood up to sing. With a skirt that was four to five inches above her knee, she aged ten years by merely standing up and revealing an unflattering feature. I found myself reducing my assessment to "She looks great for a 62-year-old woman."

Why the change in my opinion? When you dress like a younger woman, you position yourself to be compared to younger women. She had great legs for a 62-year-old woman, but carries the telltale signs of age – knobby knees!

There are many fabulous books on dressing well at any age. I will not attempt to replicate their advice, but I have listed a couple of ideas for over-50 job seekers. When in doubt, seek the advice of a professional.

Your packaging helps define the message you send to others

Companies spend millions of dollars packaging their products to ensure that their message is apparent. (It shouldn't cost you nearly that much!) Look around the house at products you have purchased, paying attention to the packaging. Ivory® Soap and Campbell's® soups have distinctive packaging. Like most products, you should be distinctively packaged, too. But what does your packaging tell consumers about the product? Are you a trusted, familiar, reliable stand-by, or a fresh, innovative breath of fresh air? Are you a classic or unpredictable? Do you project confidence and competence or uncertainty and indifference?

What does your packaging look like?

Some think of image as something shallow but as with commercial brands, personal branding includes the proper selection and construction of your "packaging."

First impressions matter. You must take control of your appearance. People form opinions of you – right or wrong – within moments of meeting you. That means you can't afford to leave someone's impression of you up to chance.

Studies show that in the first 30 seconds of meeting you, people base their impression of you on this:

55 percent	What they see
38 percent	How you speak
7 percent	What you say

We all know snap judgments can be wrong and unfair. Still, you can't ignore the reality: people form opinions based on the most minor details. More than half of what goes into forming someone's first impression of you happens even before you open your mouth. That's right: 55 percent of someone's initial response to you is based on visual cues. That could easily be a whole workbook in itself (check out **Spin Me: Creating the Image That Gets the Job; An Image Guide for Recent Grads and Job Hunters** but for the basics, here's a primer on what to consider, especially when going to an interview.

Clothing – People do judge books by their covers, every day. Make sure that *your* cover conveys the message you want people to remember. Here's a sample of messages that your clothing might be saying about you –whether you like it or not:

Tips for the 50+ job seeker

> You can't help getting older, but
> you don't have to get old."
> – George Burns, Comedian

- First and foremost, if you purchased your interview suit in the 1900s… think about an upgrade. You must look current. Your clothing, your eyewear, and your hair must tell the story that you are current. That does not mean to dress like a youngster, only that you must appear up-to-date, interesting, fresh, competent, etc. Invest in an all-weather wool suit in navy blue or charcoal gray. For creative industries, you have more latitude with color.
- **Both sexes:** Make a statement about your personality with your tie or scarf choice and/or jewelry selection. For men, think of the tie as a highway to your face. What highway is the interviewer on? Interstate (I)-boring or, I-interesting, I-creative? The tie should have a fairly small pattern so that it remains somewhat conservative; use color to tell the story. Women especially, can use jewelry to bring color and interest into the interview uniform. Earrings should not dangle and the jewelry should not make noise as it can be distracting.

- **Both sexes:** If your hair is silver, wear accents of blue or a French blue shirt to add vitality to your face. Depending on your personal coloring, a white shirt can drain the color from your face, leaving a "ghastly" appearance. If you have stark silver in your hair and the rest of your hair is black or very deep brown, avoid brown tones; the color will make your hair look dull.
- **Both sexes:** Before your interview, use Visine®. Not only does it "get the red out," it also whitens and adds a little sparkle.
- **Both sexes:** If your teeth are stained, consider professional teeth cleaning or whitening. If that's too expensive, then opt for some of the over-the-counter toothpaste whiteners.
- **Women:** Please do not wear a skirt that is above your knees to an interview. Remember: most interviews are conducted sitting down – usually without a table in front of you. When you sit, your skirt rises. The perfect length is mid-knee or, if you still have killer legs, at or just above the knee. But test it first: sit down to see how much leg is exposed to your interviewer.
- **Women:** Make sure your undergarments fit properly – no VPL (visible panty lines) and a well-fitted bra can take years off of your appearance. Consider a body shaper to eliminate "muffin top" and help correct your posture.
- **Women:** Give your face a lift by arching your eye brows (not too much though – you don't want to resemble Cruella DeVille).
- **Both sexes:** Invest in a facial or purchase your own Galvanic Spa System (visit: NuSkin.com
- **Both sexes:** Keep perfume, cologne, and aftershave to a minimum. You don't want to overpower your interviewer. Consider a fresh, light, and airy scent for daytime, or nothing at all, in case your interviewer is sensitive to scent.
- **Both sexes:** Make sure that your nails are well manicured. Apply a good moisturizer on the day of the interview to minimize lines and any blotchiness.
- **Women:** Do not wear bright-red lipstick to an interview; tone it down for the day. High-contrast colors will bring more attention to age lines around your lips.
- **Both sexes:** Your shoes should be polished, well-heeled and easy to walk in. Avoid thick rubber soles (of the orthopedic variety – unless you need them), and stilettos (just let it go).

Speaking style

If you doubt that the power and quality of a voice can make a difference in the image you project, think about James Earl Jones. What's the first thing you think of? Though he is a fine actor with a commanding presence, his greatest asset is that rich and resonant bass voice. (His voice has been immortalized as the character Darth Vader in the *Star Wars* franchise.) Not everyone has such a gift. **But everyone can work with what they have.** Use your natural voice, speaking at a normal rate and volume, without punctuating your sentences with sighs and filler sounds (e.g., "um," "well"). Vary your intonations; modulations convey your enthusiasm, interest, and comfort with the subject. Pay attention to vocal inflection (you don't want to put anyone to sleep), use clear pronunciation and enunciation, and if you have a phrase that you tend to repeat (e.g., "in fact," "to tell the truth"), try to shake the habit.

Body language

Start with a firm, sincere handshake, maintain eye contact and give a warm smile. The handshake is critical because it initiates the social contract. Whether you are going to the most important meeting of your career or not, you should come across as confident and capable. Don't stare at your shoes or, even worse, into space. Don't fidget with your hands or hide them in pockets or behind your back. **Enter the room with poise, confidence and a self-assured presence, as if the cameras are rolling and you're the star.** Once you sit down, try to appear relaxed, but don't go to extremes: no lounging back in your chair or slouching.

What about your business? Are you ready to invest in the image of your company?

> Questions to consider that will help you understand what message your marketing collateral might be sending to your clients about your business.

Is your business email address associated with a free consumer account (Gmail, Hotmail, Yahoo)? If so, what message are you sending to potential customers about your investment in your company?

Are the materials that represent your company printed on your desktop printer with perforated edges to tear off, giving the message that you just opened your company yesterday?

___

(Don't laugh, I have received "business cards" from grown folks that were printed on their computers and whose perforated edges loudly proclaim, "I'm not fully committed to this business.")

Does your material clearly state what makes you different or special – your niche – or is it so generic that it could apply to almost any business in your industry?

What evidence of excellence (e.g., testimonials, awards) are you relaying to potential customers?

CHAPTER ELEVEN

Vision — A Gift...and a Curse

A Book in Four Chapters

Chapter One: Once upon a time there was a boy who walked down a street and fell into a manhole.

Chapter Two: The boy walked down the same street, saw the manhole, yet fell in again.

Once upon a time there was a boy who walked down a street..

...and fell into a manhole.

Chapter Three: The boy walked down the same street, saw the manhole, and walked around it.

Chapter Four: The boy walked down a different street.

I don't know who wrote that "short book" with the big lesson, but its message is clear. You may easily "see" an obstacle or opportunity, but it's another thing to internalize the information and act upon it.

The boy walked down the same street, saw the manhole,

..yet fell in again.

Exploring your vision: It's a gift and a curse

You might argue that we should have started with vision. I would suggest that there is a method to the madness. If we had started with the question of vision before completing the brand work in the previous chapters, most people would have simply said, "I want to do more of the same." They would not use this opportunity to identify a bigger pie or even a new flavor of pie.

So, let's explore the question of your VISION; the ideal state you are working toward creating. If you are like most ambitious people, you are always on the move, always in pursuit of the next thing. You're moving fast and are almost always focused on the future, sometimes to a very intense degree. You barely stand still long enough to take a snapshot of your current state. That makes pinning down and defining your "vision" difficult. As the obsessive-compulsive TV detective Adrian Monk says of his incomparable powers of logic and deduction, "It's a gift...and a curse."

Let's try your vision on for size – give it a test drive. To do so, you'll write your vision statement in the present tense. **It should not be your current life, but your vision for your future, written as if it were true today.** We are declaring the future as if it were **NOW!** Let's make it clear. How do you get from THEN to NOW? VISION and ACTION!

When I think of a clear vision statement, I think of Pepsi®. For Pepsi®, the statement "Beat Coke®" creates a compelling view of the future. It is clear and concise. It does not leave much to the imagination. Anyone on the Pepsi® sales and marketing team understands the vision of the organization. Simply put, Pepsi® wants to oust the number one cola brand, Coca-Cola®, and take the number one spot.

If your goal is to find a new position or start a business and you don't have a compelling vision of where you are going, it will be difficult to line up the resources, organize your strategy, or make your goal become a reality. Once you place the stake in the ground, everything you do can then be in alignment with that vision. Writing your vision, NOW, puts your stake in the ground.

In December 2005, after 108 years of competing, the PepsiCo brand finally beat Coke®!

The boy walked down the same street, saw the manhole, and walked around it.

So, how does this information apply to your branding efforts? With any product, including ourselves, the more clearly we can summarize our goals for the future, the easier it is to craft a strategy that will enable us to begin realizing that vision.

Now, we certainly intend to reach our vision – or at least move in the direction of the vision – in less than 108 years. The point is to have a vision and then place resources and action in alignment with that vision.

The boy walked down a different street.

Marva's vision for NOW

I defined what I want: To be free. Here's how my own VISION statement will help me achieve that goal.

- My e-books and products have sold more than 100,000 units every year, bringing me financial freedom. I conduct five workshops per month either in person or as a webinar.
- I have a successful coaching practice that assists thousands of Baby Boomers in reinventing their lives.
- I have a national nonprofit organization, UXsformU, which employs at-risk and formerly incarcerated youth, giving them a fresh start, a brighter vision, and a healthy love of self. We are transforming lives. This brings me joy, which feels like emotional freedom.
- I have finally figured out how to successfully combine work and play. My speaking and consulting engagements include some of the best resorts in the world: Hawaii, France, and Brazil. Yes, I get paid well – while on vacation. I work ten hours a week and play (or network) the rest of the time.

- I am a mentor to small business owners as well as family members and friends who are starting or have started businesses. I am respected, appreciated, and fulfilled.
- In my personal life, I am balanced. I am taking care of myself in all aspects of my life: physical, spiritual, mental and emotional. And by the way…I am no longer single.

"Vision is the art of seeing the invisible." – Jonathan Swift

What is your NOW statement? Write your vision as if it were your present reality.

_____
_____
_____
_____
_____
_____
_____
_____
_____
_____
_____
_____
_____
_____
_____
_____
_____
_____
_____
_____

"Don't underestimate the power of a vision. McDonald's founder Ray Kroc pictured his empire long before it existed, and he saw how to get there. He invented the company motto – 'Quality, service, cleanliness and value' and kept repeating it to employees for the rest of his life."
– Kenneth Labich, Business Guru

"Peak performers want more than merely to win the next game. They see all the way to the championship. They have a long-range goal that inspires commitment and action."
– Charles Garfield, Peak Performer

CHAPTER TWELVE

You Can't Get from THEN to NOW without ACTION

Copyright, Marva Goldsmith & Associates, Inc

October 13

As you know, I promised myself that I would do something significant each month until my December birthday. In October, I made a significant purchase. It cost $3,000.

His name is Adam.

Now, before your mind starts to wander in the wrong direction, Adam is a branding expert who focuses on media. For my budget, Adam represents a very healthy investment – one that demonstrates my commitment to achieving my NOW state.

How committed are you to your vision? How much are you willing to invest to make it happen?

Many people will read this workbook. Some will complete the exercises; others may even feel motivated to pursue a new career or start a business and make plans to go into action. But only a precious few will actually put resources behind their plans and take the first steps toward realizing their vision. **You can't get from THEN to NOW without ACTION!**

My pet rock – make that e-rock!

As a baby boomer and entrepreneur, I have high regard for Gary Dahl, the inventor of the Pet Rock. The Pet Rock was a plain old rock, nothing special – until it was marketed as a pet. It was sold in a cardboard box that looked like a pet carrying case. It contained a training manual with topics like, "How to House-train your Pet Rock." The rock, which sold in the 70s for $3.95, was featured in *Newsweek*, sold in outlets all over the country, including Neiman Marcus, and eventually earned Dahl a coveted spot on *The Tonight Show* with Johnny Carson. For me, the success of the Pet Rock is a constant reminder that all things are possible.

One facet of my NOW vision state is to become an Internet millionaire. The Internet is the only vehicle I know of that, with a good product and proper marketing strategy, can help you create wealth literally overnight. *Can I sell 100,000 units each year at a profit margin of $10 a piece on the Internet?*

By accomplishing this goal, I will then have the capital to fund my nonprofit, and spend my Golden Years experiencing the world...*Free to roam the country.*

In My Experience...

While I did not experience a layoff, I felt a groundswell of emotions when leaving the traditional organizational life I had known for more than 30 years. I desired a new career direction that would give me a greater sense of purpose and fulfillment. I had always envisioned myself a consultant and college instructor after retirement. This opportunity presented itself earlier than planned so I seized it without hesitation.

In order to teach at the university level, I knew it would require a terminal degree. In 2003, I began planning to pursue a doctorate degree. Five years later, I completed my Doctor of Psychology Degree in Organization Development and Consulting Psychology. During the period I was in school, I maintained my consulting practice and a full-time job.

After graduation, I began to pursue my career interest. I posted my resume and CV on career websites, attended a few career fairs directed at the teaching profession, and asked for several information gathering interviews which were extremely helpful.

To what specifically do you attribute your success? Having a clear, concise plan and executing it were key factors in my success. The educational preparation process was the primary goal because without it, the plan would not have been effective. After I completed the degree, I was blessed to receive adjunct teaching offers at two institutions. After teaching one term at The Chicago School of Professional Psychology, I was offered a full-time position as Lead Faculty for the Industrial and Organizational Psychology Department and as an Associate Professor. It was truly a fortuitous case of preparation and opportunity meeting at a predestined moment in time (not a coincidence).

What lessons or insights would you share with others in a similar position? If you have a dream you must convert that dream into a **personal strategic plan with specific goals and action steps**. If you are unsure about what you want to do or how to do it, seek out assistance by speaking to career counselors or life coaches. The bottom-line is, no one will make your dreams come true *for* you! Nothing has ever replaced hard work and determination to achieve life's goals; it all begins with a plan.

How is your new job different from what you have done in the past, if at all? This job (career) is entirely different from anything I have ever done in the past. While it is different, there were numerous transferrable skills I was able to bring to the position. I believe a complete skills inventory is vital and should be a key factor when reinventing one's self. I was able to indentify the skills I was lacking very early in the process and, when I realized I was deficient in certain areas, I made it a point to incorporate those development needs into my graduate education.

Is there anything else that you want to share with others or words of wisdom? We must always keep moving in the direction of our goals. We are going to experience set-backs in life – that's a given. Nonetheless, the path forward is what will get us to that state of fulfillment with respect to our accomplishments. There's no more exhilarating feeling than knowing you've realized one of your life's dreams!

Dr. Albert Edwards, III
Los Angeles, CA
Age 53

November 1

My November birthday gift will not cost me anything. This month I will spend time renewing relationships, putting people first, and just enjoying the journey.

What a gift!

CHAPTER THIRTEEN

Social Media Revolution

Don't be scared! Make social media your new best friend

When the first edition of this book was written, I had only just begun to utilize social marketing as a tool. The tool has been so fantastic I have to share what I have learned with you. Note that this section of the book will become obsolete even before the book is printed. In fact, I believe that having a social media strategy is so important that I have begun working on an online brand strategist certification. Check out my website for more information, (marvagoldsmith.com or branding50.com)

In the 21st century we are seeing the most amazing technological, informational, and social revolution ever with Web 2.0 social media (interactive online communication), including Internet marketing opportunities available for everyone to optimize. Incredibly, social networking options are free at the entry-level, making them excellent and cost-effective marketing tools for job search and business marketing strategies. Social media is not limited to young folks, but enables everyone to facilitate communication with live human beings across space and time zones.

That's why if you're actively engaged in a branding effort in search of a new job or to expand business leads, you'll need to learn, join, and use social networking opportunities to continually reinvent and freshen up your brand image and expertise in the face of fluctuating economic and social conditions.

Occasionally, I have asked friends, "Are you on Facebook?" They look at me the way some people look at older women in mini-skirts and *too* much makeup and say, "No. My kids are." If you are reading this book, chances are likely that your age is in the vicinity of 50. If you think Facebook and Twitter are only for your kids… please reassess your position.

If it seems like an overwhelming proposition, take baby steps:

- **Use social networking to keep in touch with friends and family first.** I am now in touch with people that I have not seen, talked to, and in some cases, even thought about in 30 years. It has been wonderful to just check in with them, occasionally comment on something they have posted, or provide an unexpected lead or share information from which they might benefit.
- **Develop a visible and credible online profile to create social media that will enhance your online-branding effort.** Some sites are more personal than business, but always be aware of the image projected by the photos you post (or are posted by others).
- **If you're a job-seeker or business owner, branding and expanding your online image and presence is an essential component for effective networking.**
- **Understand that if you are going into business and you do not have an online presence, the absence of information is also a part of your brand…**the lack of data is then your brand instead.

After gaining confidence in these areas, you'll ask yourself (like I did), "Why didn't I join social sites like Face-book, LinkedIn, and Twitter (I'm still working on this one) sooner?"

The twin goals of this chapter are to show you how easy it is:

- To get familiar with social networking
- To put into practice your own social networking strategy for free. What have you got to lose?

Let me share my story. I signed up with LinkedIn® (the leading social site for professional and business people) in December 2004 purely to stop friends from bugging me about joining. You've probably received some of these emails, too. I joined, and it took me two years to understand the importance of creating a credible profile. Over the next two years, I would build my network to 177 connections. Collectively, these 177 connections have over 56,800 connections. LinkedIn® allows you access to the third level of business connections. In my case, I now have access to over 4 million people (by introduction from the first and second level of connections). I have not even begun to use this feature.

I recognize these vast numbers as potential – people with different ideas, different experiences and untapped genius. Soon after joining, I purchased a book called, "*You're on LinkedIn, Now What?*" I realized that I should try to understand how to optimize the power of this network. I read one chapter at a time, and did exactly what the author suggested. The chapter called *Groups* was of particular interest to me because I have always believed in the "power of group genius" and the ability to expand one's reach and breadth by engaging others in your work. I joined 30 affinity groups.

The first set of groups that I joined was for organizations that I belong to such as Michigan State University and Harvard Kennedy School alumni, Crain's 40 Under 40…you get the picture. Then I joined issue-related groups: human resources, baby boomer, training and consulting.

Here are a few examples of how I worked with my new best friends:

As I mention in Chapter Six, part of my branding strategy is to become more visible to human resource professionals. In June 2009, the Society of Human Resource Management (SHRM) selected me to present on the first day of this prestigious annual conference. My time slot was at 7:00 a.m. Of course, I was concerned about whether anyone would actually show up. I posted a question on LinkedIn® to my human resources groups (over 10,000 people).

This is my first time speaking at the National SHRM Conference (Monday, June 28 at 7:00 a.m.). The topic is personal branding. Do you plan to attend the conference? Any suggestions? Please join me.

My plea for company received responses with suggestions from about 20 people, and a handful of people promised to attend my "early riser" session on Personal Branding. I do not know how many people read the question, or how many showed up as a result of this invitation, but I had made my first foray into tapping the power of the LinkedIn® group function.

After publishing my book, *Branding Yourself After Age 50: Creating Brand Strategy for Life*, to celebrate my rite of passage when I turned 50 in

December 2008, I posed a question to the baby boomer group members (about 1,000 people):

> *I recently published a book titled, Branding Yourself After Age 50. Other than AARP, do you have any suggestions for conferences/venues where I can speak about personal branding and/or sell my books? Thank you.*

The floodgates opened to reveal amazing leads – as if I'd struck oil. From this question, I received about 35 responses ranging from suggestions on associations and websites to people I should contact. Most impressively, one response led to a radio interview in Sacramento, California, (Living Well Radio NewsTalk 1530 KFBK) and another led to conducting two webinars for Georgetown University alumni. In addition, I was invited to present a workshop for a 50+ networking group in Michigan, which would provide me with my first book signing event. I felt like a star! The amazing thing is that these leads and opportunities were **all from people who had never laid their eyes on me** – with the exception of my profile picture.

It should be obvious now why I had to write this section to share the good news about social networking. It is a must – especially for the 50 and over crowd. You will not be alone. Learn how to tap into **the power of unlimited group genius.**

There is also the other side of the coin, which is *answering* questions. When you begin to share your expertise with others, you are branding yourself online as an expert in your field. But make sure that the information provided is correct! I look for opportunities to provide the same exceptional experience to others that I continue to enjoy with my new best friends.

So, what is "Web 2.0" social media?

The most astounding invention of the 21st century is undoubtedly Web 2.0 social media. Why? Web 2.0 allows everyone free platforms to build their own weblogs. Web 1.0 accesses information from traditional websites built at great cost by web designers and programmers. With DIY (do-it-yourself) interactive Web 2.0, however, YOU write and control your own weblog (as the term indicates, it's a contraction of "website" and "blog"), updating and spinning info without having to learn computer code, or hire an expensive programmer. Web 2.0 enables easy interaction with people from across the globe.

Do you see why DIY Web 2.0 social media is a communication revolution that's also social in promoting contact based on an ever-growing foundation of trustworthy friends? You are in complete control of what you want to share with them and the www – whole wide world – through your own weblog!

Benefits to Job Seekers:

- Posting a professional profile of your experiences, names of contacts for references, volunteer projects, awards and other pertinent info on your blog for easy access.
- Posting a video resume for prospective employers "to meet" you on YouTube. Type in "video resume" to see what other job seekers are doing.

Benefits to Business Owners:

- Posting a company profile with a description of services and related info on your weblog.
- Posting info-filled blogs (also known as articles) at least twice weekly as lead-ins to your website.
- Ongoing opportunities to target thousands and possibly millions of sales leads!

Why is social media so effective?

- Especially in an age of "social disconnect," it's an engaging way to feel connected and to find new friends, or reacquaint yourself with old friends.
- Your "friends" are already pre-selected by the nature of the social sites you join.
- You enjoy the convenience of just a few clicks that allow you to reach employers and prospects, which saves time and money – not to mention going green and saving resources.

- Best of all, membership is free at the entry-level. The sites are self-sustaining with add-ons and higher levels of membership for purchase if you so wish.

Whether you're on a mission to hunt down a good-fit job regardless of the economy or seeking to expand your business by generating free leads, you've got to learn the true value of grasping and applying DIY social media. Begin by blogging.

Go to www.youtube.com and type in, "How do I create a blog?" Or, go to www.wordpress.org for easy, how-to steps to download their free software to get started. Write Search Engine Optimized articles to position yourself as a thought leader in your field.

I am conducting webinars – interactive online workshops that are a variation of social networking for professional training. Hosted by Maestro Conference, http://maestroconference.com, these webinars are very different from traditional teleseminars. Participants break up into smaller groups, interact with and learn from each other, and return to main seminar sessions – all from Internet convenience.

Participants will be given an opportunity to meet like-minded individuals, share ideas, and network in a dynamic environment that combines the convenience of traditional conference calls with the interactivity of a live workshop. The only thing missing is the parking fee and the ability to see and touch your neighbor. However, if a connection is made during the webinar series, participants may exchange contact information.

What about Twitter?

Twitter is the micro-blogging service that limits each post to 140 characters. It's a great way to learn effective and efficient editing while communicating clearly. My friend Karen Batchelor, a life coach and Internet marketer, has her own website about Twitter™ at www.tweetlifeblog.com. Her story is an amazing one.

"I went from ground zero to having 5,633 Twitter™ followers in six months," Karen told me. It helps that Karen's a member of multiple social-sites. "Facebook laid the foundation for me. From there I joined LinkedIn and then Twitter," she said.

Karen's tips to Twitter success

Twitter is a great tool to brand your unique capabilities and experiences, with the potential to keep growing "followers" eager to learn from you. Here are Karen's tips to imprint a knock-out Twitter brand.

- Keep your posts helpful and useful. That's how you make friends and followers eager to learn from you – info that's entertaining and inspirational.
- As soon as you sign on, immediately post an engaging bio – in 140 characters.
- Highlight your first three points as a professional and end the last point on a personal note, preferably humorous. Karen's bio is "Lawyer, former corporate exec now certified coach BIG into helping you achieve a transformational career or midlife makeover."
- Experiment with and create an online color brand. Go to a fabric store and drape different colored fabrics for a backdrop to see which color best reflects your personality. Use this color to develop your online brand. (Karen's is a rich, vibrant red, as you can see.)
- Use a flattering current photo.
- Instead of using a stock Twitter background, which immediately announces you're a newbie, customize one that's different and unique to you.
- Pick a user name you're comfortable with, something like a pen name.
- For your background info, give three items – favorite books, movies, etc.
- As an analogy, Karen says she'd rather not have company if her house is not yet looking its best – so, in the same manner, prepare and create your Twitter brand before signing on.

I hope this section has been helpful to you. There are so many resources available on the web. Don't overlook this important tool in your networking toolkit. Get over your reticence quickly. If you haven't joined a social site yet, you're missing out on a social revolution of global proportions that's unlike any. By quantum leaps and bounds you can expand your knowledge and possibly your career and business success.

But, Can Social Media Really Help You Find a Job?

> "Personal branding serves as career protection in uncertain times. It's also a critical tool for reinventing yourself because you can leverage the reputation and skill set you already have to prove you have the ability to do the job you want."
> Dan Schawbel, Author, Me 2.0

I met Deborah Porter online. Deborah is a part of the 632 friends and colleagues that I am connected to – that provide me access to a network of more than eight million people – on the social media site, LinkedIn. Huge network, eh?

I had never communicated with the inspiring Deborah Porter until I read about her recent accomplishment of finding a job by using social networking on LinkedIn.

Deborah's Story

I am 50 years old. I had been unemployed for six months. I created the LinkedIn connection to keep in contact with people I had built a professional relationship with in my old job as the Director of Social Marketing. Previously, I worked in Erie County, New York, on a grant for an organization called Family Voices Network. After the grant ended, I joined the chorus of the unemployed.

I felt a need to reinvent myself and, at age 50, recognized that would begin with my gray hair. A colleague suggested that I dye my hair. So I did.

I planned to start consulting as a social marketing specialist and created a website to highlight my professional successes (www.wobblee.com). Soon afterwards *(within 30 days after sending an invitation to join my LinkedIn connection),* I was picked up as an Associated Faculty Member by the Center for Community Leadership and worked with the organization to provide social marketing training, combined with their leadership training.

I began to network on LinkedIn by participating in discussion groups, webinars, Q&A, etc. Prior to LinkedIn I had never used a social media site before, but I learned that I could create a Twitter account and started sending some of my Updates from LinkedIn to Twitter. Through networking on

LinkedIn, my network grew to 276 people, with 12 recommendations that strengthened my profile. Through my participation in the various groups, I became engaged with my new circle of friends. If I saw a topic that interested me, I responded.

The Job

One of my contacts on LinkedIn (new best friend) read my profile and suggested that I would be a good fit for the organization. I was already familiar with the organization while in my old job. To my surprise, they thought I was already working and when they discovered I was consulting, invited me to come in for an interview.

The Search

At my age, I found that many organizations want top talent but are only willing to pay entry-level salaries and that's why I was reinventing myself. At one point, I thought I'd have to downgrade tremendously to an administrative assistant position and create two resumes: one for community outreach/marketing and another for administrative assistant work. It would have been a coin toss. What I discovered while unemployed is that the administrative assistant position was the most likely available job in my market. Needless to say, it's been a journey and I've been very fortunate in this economy to find work in my chosen field of expertise.

The LinkedIn profile was my top lead and I posted my resume on the site as well as Monster, CareerBuilder, Jobs.com and a few others. Although many of the positions on Monster.com fit my skill set, it was difficult to get noticed. I did everything that a job coach would suggest – sent cover letters tailored to the job description, ensured that the resume highlighted what they were looking for, and provided links to my website for credibility, etc. LinkedIn was the most beneficial in the long run. It offers a professional network of people and an opportunity to engage on a variety of different levels. Additionally, during tough economic times, LinkedIn helped me to stay in touch with other professionals, to gain knowledge on social media that I added to my toolbox, and LinkedIn allowed for the participation in discussion groups that kept my skills fresh and creative juices flowing.

The Internet was also helpful in providing good information about salary negotiation: visit cbsalary.com (a CareerBuilder website) and salary.com. I also read a link in a blog that provided excellent techniques on how to negotiate for your salary. From there, I used the search engines to find other information on salary negotiation. Now I was ready and confident about negotiating my salary. I began to understand how people in my position could easily price themselves out of a job when employers asked, "What salary are you looking for?" By reading this information I was able to position myself better when asked about the salary requirements. Although I felt the salary that I was offered undercut my level of experience, I accepted the position and asked if there was room for negotiation and requested a meeting with the Executive Director to discuss. I wanted this position because it was a perfect fit but I also wanted to be compensated for my skills and experience. The salary offered was for an entry-level person.

I went to the second interview to discuss the criteria of the written job description, gain a better understanding of what they wanted from me, and demonstrate how I could help their organization. Then, we developed a plan to address what they really wanted from the job description. As a result, the job description changed and I negotiated a substantial salary increase of $6,000 after the probationary period.

Not being afraid to ask the questions after presenting what I could specifically do for the organization (Unique Selling Proposition) gave me the strength to just "put it out there" with confidence. After all, what do you have to lose?

Deborah Porter is the Community Outreach Specialist at Read to Succeed Buffalo, Inc., a literacy organization that promotes and supports literacy initiatives within the City of Buffalo.

CHAPTER FOURTEEN

Ready, Camera, ACTION!

Copyright, Marva Goldsmith & Associates, Inc

Power-filled actions!

So, this is it! It's all about action.

In a second you can take charge, develop a new path, and create a new chapter. Plan to accomplish some small feat every day. By the end of the month, you will have taken 30 steps towards your goal.

What are you willing to do in the next week to bring your vision into reality? Why one week? Because life happens one week, one day, one minute, one second at a time. In one week you can change the trajectory of your life. In one week you can realize a shift and chart measurable progress towards your goal.

Get into the habit of setting weekly Power Goals. The small changes will begin to shape your future. The vision that was once far away becomes closer and you reinvent yourself one Power-filled week at a time.

Your Power Goals should be SMART: **S**pecific, **M**easurable, **A**chievable, **R**ealistic, and **T**ime-based. That way you can return to the plan and determine fairly quickly if the goals were accomplished. And *NO, you do not get to rest on Sunday*. Instead, on that "day of rest," conduct a **15-minute** action towards accomplishing the week's goal or develop your power plan for next week.

Here's a sample One-Week Power Plan for Art, who decided on a writing career after parting ways with his corporate managerial position. We will check in later to see what actions were taken within the week and what resulted from taking those actions.

Art's One-Week Power Plan

Three actions could move him toward his desired brand:

- **Goal 1:** Improve turnaround of project elements, installments, or revisions to no more than 48 hours.
- **Goal 2:** Send email follow-ups to all prospective Guru.com employers whose projects I have bid on but have not received a reply.
- **Goal 3:** Write holiday cards to send to all of my clients as a means of keeping in touch and establishing an ongoing rapport.

Here is Art's score for the week:
- **Goal 1:** I turned around two of my writing assignments within 48 hours, even over Thanksgiving Day. However, on a couple of others I exceeded the 48-hour turnaround time limit. This was partly due to my obligation to work holiday overtime hours at my retail job, which is not an excuse, but it was a factor.
- **Goal 2:** I sent follow-up notes to all five prospective Guru.com employers whose projects I have bid on; I received no replies, but the projects are still listed as "open" on the bid tracking page.
- **Goal 3:** My holiday cards are written out, signed, enveloped, stamped and ready to mail out later this week.

COACH'S NOTE:

How did you feel about your Power Goals? What results did you realize?

What I have learned from this Power Goals exercise – and indeed, from what Marva has been saying to me all along – is that *decisive and direct action* is necessary for success.

As part of this exercise, after only five follow-up letters to prospective Guru.com employers whose posted projects I had bid on, I have had a response from one who wants me to ghostwrite his book for him – and that was a posting that had expired. I could have written it off, and instead, the follow-up landed me the job!

Now, what more motivation for direct and decisive action could I possibly need? I believe I can say for a certainty that I am motivated enough to believe I can and will do better on my Power Plan for next week, and the week after that, and the week after that.

Coach's Nudge:

On the next page, write your Power Plan. Please take the challenge to change the trajectory of your life by writing your plan down. It starts with this one small step. Remember: these are measurable goals that you will accomplish within the course of a week and that are facets of your larger goal.

Reward success

If you are working with a partner or as a book club, hold a small celebration next week to acknowledge each person as they announce the **WOW** (Within One Week) accomplishments that I'm sure they will have!

> Make copies of the next page, or create your own way to record and track your weekly Power Plan.

YOUR POWER PLAN Week of _____

LEADERSHIP

What did you accomplish this week?

_____
_____
_____
_____
_____
_____
_____
_____
_____
_____
_____
_____
_____
_____
_____
_____
_____
_____
_____
_____
_____
_____
_____
_____
_____
_____

VISIBILITY

What did you accomplish this week?

_____
_____
_____
_____
_____
_____
_____
_____
_____
_____
_____
_____
_____
_____
_____
_____
_____
_____
_____
_____
_____
_____
_____
_____
_____
_____
_____

CONSISTENCY

What did you accomplish this week?

Notes

In My Experience...

In January 2009, I was laid off from my position as General Manager at ITW/Auto Wax. The company went through a corporate downsizing. More than anything it was scary. I think I knew intellectually the job market was bad, but I had a very stable job history and had never had a problem finding a position in the past.

My wife and I drastically cut back our living expenses.

I went to work learning about online networking and social media. I filled out my LinkedIn profile that had been basically inactive. I created a Facebook page, a Twitter account, started a blog and created a website.

After 3 months of looking and not finding another full time job, I finally woke up and realized that what I was bringing in was contract accounting work and tax work. I stopped looking for a job and focused my efforts on marketing myself as a CPA. I now have over 4,500 followers (@rivescpa) on Twitter and picked up six new clients in 2009 from my efforts.

Most people want to be referred to a CPA or know them personally. How did you develop the trust online? How did you create a compelling enough brand online to get business? The majority of my new business came directly or indirectly through social media efforts. I developed relationships with other people and groups who are active online, especially those involved with small businesses which is my niche market. Providing useful information and participating in online networking groups were helpful. I often answered small business and/or tax questions online.

An online community works much like a real community where you develop relationships with people who will refer business to you and, in fact, being readily available online broadened my geographic market reach. I have gained new clients outside of Dallas and even outside of Texas by being «virtually» available.

Most of the growth of my online community has been organic. I have listed myself on Twellow and put the link to my Twitter profile on most of my other social media profiles. People find me by searching Google and referrals from other contacts. http://rives-cpa.com

To what specifically do you attribute your success? I spent the previous five years in a primarily sales and marketing position rather than just a financial position. It taught me a lot more about how to sell myself.

What lessons or insights would you share with others in a similar position? Have at least an idea of what your long term objectives are, but be open to any opportunity that comes along and don't automatically say no to anything.

How is your new job different from what you have done in the past, if at all? Now it is truly up to me to make things happen and keep the bills paid.

What are the largest changes that have occurred as a result of your new position? I no longer believe in the security of climbing the corporate ladder. I now believe you have to make your own opportunities to advance your career.

What advice would you give or did you receive that was most helpful throughout the changes you made? Finding a job where you make a career out of working at one place for 10-20 years does not exist anymore. Businesses no longer feel loyalty to their employees and the younger generation of workers have adapted to that and they no longer feel loyalty to their employer. Not that they don't do good work; but they don't mind using one company as a stepping stone to something better and will readily jump at a better opportunity.

Is there anything else that you want to share with others or words of wisdom? Don't be afraid of change, because it will happen. Not only do things change, but the pace at which things change is constantly increasing today.

Wray Rives
Coppell, TX
Age: 52

You have read many examples of people who, after age 50, have re-charged a stalled career, started a new business, or placed new energy in a lost passion simply by engaging branding principles.

Are you still not convinced that the possibilities are endless? Please meet a few more of my friends.

What I Did For Love: The Quest of a Lifelong Learner

It is a myth that we learned all we need to know in Kindergarten – at least I did not. At age 50, I decided to return to school to complete a master's degree. I was already a successful consultant earning a respectable salary, but I had an undeniable urge to continue the acquisition of knowledge. I enjoy reading, writing, researching, intellectual debates, and experiential activities, so pursuing a master's degree was the next logical thing to do. Why not?

On May 11, 2008, at age 53, I listened to the Honorable Vernon Jordan deliver the American University Commencement address, anticipating my walk across the stage to receive my Master of Science Degree in Organization Development (MSOD). I was seated strategically so that I could glimpse the smiling faces of my mother and father, both 70-years plus, who had traveled by train from Connecticut to be present. It was Mother's Day and what better gift could I give my parents, both of whom were obliged to forsake college to work and raise a family. Clapping loudly also were my two daughters, Camille and Celeste, 13 and 12 years old respectively. Later in the day, they shared with me their ideas and prospects for which universities they might attend to be "just like mom." They reminded me often that they deserved some credit and recognition on this occasion. It was true; they often accompanied me to the library to study and they helped me on several class projects.

Lovingly, I gazed upon Calvin, my husband of 15 years, who had picked up the slack and maintained the home front during my many years of part-time collegiate life. He was a faithful proofreader of my school papers, and a reluctant guinea pig for me to test the theories and concepts I was digesting. Calvin often jokingly remarked that he was "attending sixth grade and eighth grade with my daughters and graduate school with my wife – all simultaneously, without the rewards."

My cousin from New Jersey, Michele Amad, a 2006 graduate of Rutgers University, was the official "seat saver" and photographer on this special day. The graduation ceremony was long, and it allowed ample time for me to reflect on both the glory in my story as well as the bumps, twists, roadblocks, detours, and near fatal occurrences over the past three years. It is only fair that I share the full picture of how I earned my robe and tassel on this day.

In retrospect, I wish someone had offered me "the inside scoop" or a "back to school cheat sheet" as I embarked on this learning quest, but no "guide-book" was available. First, I must confess that I've been down this road before. I was just nine hours short of a Master of International Communication Degree from American University, class of 1993. But my education gave way to love, dating, engagement, marriage, and then children. The graduate credit hours lapsed, the degree requirements changed, the communication market shifted, and my interest abated, although only temporarily. But as it turned out, this was fortunate.

There is something about defeat that invigorates me to try even harder when given a second chance. This time my approach to graduate studies was methodical, intentional, and full of determination. In the months prior to my 50th birthday, I spent hours thinking and praying about what I wanted to do in the second half of my life. I am adept at reinventing myself, having already held many unrelated positions of ever-increasing responsibility in corporate America, always parlaying my old skills and gaining new ones to move to the next level. I now wanted to have the credentials to add credibility in the marketplace to certify my capabilities and worth.

My motivation for returning to school was selfish. I knew I needed to "keep it fresh" and update my professional toolkit in order to compete with all the smart Generation X and Y folks now in the workplace. Finances for school were not an obstacle because I was willing and able to secure needed student loans ($40K as it turned out). My desire to learn did not depend upon what others thought, what the immediate return on investment would be, or how hard the endeavor itself would be. I had an unfulfilled, lifelong-learner's dream and a deep desire to attain a master's degree. This was just as important to me as the lifestyle and income that I had achieved and naturally wanted to maintain.

Over the course of a few months, I visited several local graduate school open houses, evaluated the program options, and weighed the pros and cons of traditional night classes versus a weekend, cohort program. I selected the latter because it was easier for me to plan and block the time on my calendars, both at home and at work. That program was also designed to be more "user-friendly" for the mature working professional – no GRE or GMAT entrance tests required. Executive programs value work experiences, as working professionals are the norm. The hardest part of the admissions process was writing the personal statement explaining why this course of study and degree pursuit was important to me. Passion, energy, and commitment in my heart were my personal selling points. I had to "begin with the end in mind" and with the unwavering resolve not to give up, no matter what.

I started graduate school in June 2005, with Cohort 52, at American University/National Training Laboratories. The class began with 12 fellow cohort members, ranging in age from 24 to 55. I was not the oldest class member, but I was the only person married with young children. I realized at the onset of our course work that it took me twice as long to write a paper or complete an assignment as some of my younger cohort members. I attributed it to rusty brain cells; on the bright side, I believed the research and the intense intellectual rigor would help fend off any onset of Alzheimer's disease. This was nothing new really, as I have always had to try harder to prove myself equally competent to others in the room – I was just a little older and wiser now.

All of my friends and professional colleagues share stories about our constant struggles to "do it all," to balance work and personal life. When I initially considered adding school to the mix of an already action-packed agenda I knew it would be a challenge, but I could not have anticipated the breadth and depth of the mental and physical pain I was choosing to embrace as a "wannabe" graduate student. I was already wearing many hats – wife, mother, stepmom, daughter, daughter-in-law, friend…how hard could it be to add one more? Admittedly, I underestimated the answer to this question.

Fortunately, my employer, a large management consulting firm, is supportive of advanced education and offers generous tuition reimbursement, as well as flexible work schedules, to accommodate external training and education. However, I also had to temporarily remove myself from the consultant fast-track at the company. I was able to meet my client demands and billable hour targets, but I had to forego many extra-curricular networking and career enhancing opportunities. I could not work late or accept demanding tight-deadline assignments, such as writing proposals. I declined partner-driven special projects and highly visible tasks if they were unpredictable in scope. I elected to assume an "under the radar" profile for the three years I was in graduate school. At the end of the journey I emerged as a better consultant, but there were professional sacrifices along the way.

At home, I became comfortable with a less than "hospital clean" house, piles of unopened mail, doing less entertaining, and more dining on fast-food meals in the evenings because I did not have the time to devote to my usual duties.

Yes, I felt guilty and overwhelmed.

I developed an unhealthy routine of only four to five hours of sleep nightly, so I could study after everyone went to bed. I had an addiction to daily *venti* Starbucks in order to cope and keep the adrenaline flowing. My personal needs were ignored; I did not have time for exercise or friends. I prayed a lot and I know that it was the grace of God and my faith in His Son, Jesus Christ, which brought me over the graduate school mountain.

I missed some important occasions, such as graduations, baby christenings, weddings, and other celebrations due to the demands of school. I used every favor and chit anyone in my support group would allow, as I needed a lot of help to stay the course. I nicknamed these dedicated family and friends "my tail wind." They were all with me in spirit as I sat in the American University auditorium on graduation day. I know I could not have made the journey without them.

I am proud to be a lifelong learner and I invite you to join me in feeding the mind and soul with the ceaseless pursuit of knowledge. A master's degree is only one marker of achievement, only one form of recognition. There are so many other valuable opportunities for learning that carry their own significant rewards, both tangible and intangible.

As a mature student, there is an added feeling of accomplishment and satisfaction in gaining new skills and competencies. I would not mind if history remembers me in the same way that Grandma Moses is remembered – as a role model who successfully started a career in the arts at an advanced age and flourished. I am already secretly thinking about when I can start my Ph.D. studies.

"Dr. Carla Dancy Smith" is possible, and so is your educational dream – whatever it may be. Go for it – and be willing to sacrifice to achieve your goal!

Carla Dancy Smith
Silver Spring, MD
Age 55

Coach's Tip:

Educational information is readily available online, in libraries, community colleges, seminars, webinars, professional associations, and even through employers and peers. Learning can take place anyplace and anytime these days, virtually and independently as well as in traditional classroom programs.

Fifty and Fabulous, Darling... Choosing and Meeting the Challenge of a Lifetime

The first Saturday in June 2004; the air smells early morning fresh and the bright shining sun is a sharp contrast to my glum mood. My 50th birthday is five months away and what do I have to show for it? I fire up the car and wait for the metal parking lot gate to open. At 50 I should be a master at something. I'm on the way to the gym, my sanctuary of iron and sweat. My five-day-a-week workout has kept me sane, balanced, and lean for 25 years. This morning, however, I am neither balanced nor lean. I'm dissatisfied with the twenty-two plus pounds of extra fat that hides the proof of my five-day-a week routine. *Don't worry, girl, that lean and muscular body you've always had is underneath.* I am not consoled. "Underneath" is the operative word. It's underneath. I'm underneath. I'm hiding the mastery. The traffic light turns green as I guide my car down the ramp onto Detroit's John C. Lodge Expressway. *A bodybuilding contest... Yes! I'll do a bodybuilding contest to celebrate my 50th birthday!* The thought hits me like a ton of wonder as I accelerate and merge into traffic. I laugh out loud. It's perfect! Without a clue as to the enormity of the challenge or how profound the discoveries will be, I embark.

Soon I discover my relationship to the gym, working out, and my life. Over the years, going to the gym and working out has deteriorated into a mindless habit, much like my life. I'm bored, uninspired, and driven mostly by anxiety and fear. I'm afraid that if I miss a day, the fat monster will creep up and devour me in pounds and pounds of Häagen-Dazs Butter Pecan misery and guilt. The idea of competing in a bodybuilding contest gives me a new way to think about the gym, my workouts, and my life. I'm excited. I want to know what's underneath the layers. What's possible if I go the extra mile into the realm of excellence? Training and excellence are added to my vocabulary. They become my approach to this higher purpose. No more workouts; I'm in training for my 50s.

My weakest muscle is my relationship to food. I need discipline and perhaps a small miracle when it comes to certain foods. I love Häagen-Dazs Butter Pecan ice cream, Snickers Bars and Lay's Barbecue Potato Chips. Oprah calls it "comfort food" and "emotional eating," but I call it, "just can't eat one." Fifty *is* emotional, damn it! Suddenly, I'm hit with another thought. I've been substituting food for faith. I lack faith. Whoa! Until that moment, faith had been an unexamined frontier. Faith lived in my mind as a vague concept, an airy-fairy superstition at best. Things worked out because I was lucky, crossed my fingers, wished, hoped, prayed, and bargained with God. Food helped me endure the uncertainty while I waited and wondered if my hope would turn out. What I feared was the other side of faith, the devastating disappointment when things didn't turn out as I had hoped.

Being no stranger to disappointment, I know that it is very expensive. Disappointment costs time, money, and forward movement. The desire to bail out often, but not always, follows and that brings even more disappointment. The bodybuilding contest comes with a deadline; it's five months and one week before my 50th birthday. With no time to waste, I must move forward with discipline and faith. I struggle with discipline around food, moving forward with a clean diet, then backward with undisciplined eating. Back and forth, back and forth, no net gain.

Discipline and faith become practices that move me forward. Discipline gets me to the gym and on the treadmill by 7:00 a.m. Faith is in the application of three sets of fifteen focused reps for each muscle group in my body. Discipline is in the six small, clean, meals I eat each day. Faith is the investment in my personal trainer. He won't allow me to wallow in disappointments, setbacks, or beat myself up and waste time with a "poor me" attitude. My excitement leads me to join a community of bodybuilding folks; I learn more than anyone needs to know about diet, weight training, nutrition, vitamins, supplements, and yes, discipline.

Discipline becomes a form of love. Love points me to my future. Discipline is in the steps I take to get there and faith is the guarantee that I will arrive. This way to success, that way to setback and failure, the choice is mine every single day. Faith travels light. Criticism and judgment is extra baggage. Faith allows me to take only the lessons from my choices. Discipline encourages me to make the more powerful choice.

After the first month, the weight loss is evident and I'm encouraged. The second month I'm bursting with energy. I can see the fat melt away to reveal the muscle cuts. Highly motivated, I chant a new mantra, "No fat between me and God." I feel like a sculptor and my body is the marble. Burning fat, building muscle, and being very disciplined around diet and exercise are my chiseling tools. To neglect any one of these areas is to be out of sync with my goal and intention. By month three, I'm a machine. Foods outside of my committed goal are no longer relevant. I feel great! People stop and ask, "Are you a dancer?" "How did you get your arms like that?" Strangers want to touch my biceps and my niece wants to be like me when she grows up. Only 10 percent of people go where I am going. I become an anonymous spokeswoman for health and fitness in the circles I travel.

My trainer and I attend a few bodybuilding contests to see what they're like and what to expect. It's a different world that has its own unique rules, regulations, and smells that permeate the auditorium or theatre: boiled eggs, sun-bathed, tanned bodies wearing bronzers, chocolate, Pam® Cooking Spray and other oils to show the body to best effect under the lights. It's a world of competing bodies, where the healthiest, most muscular, most symmetrical and graceful are crowned king and queen. The parade of the top 10 percent of bodies is breathtaking. The posing suits are spectacular and the contest is entertaining.

After observing all the categories, I decide to compete in the figure category. This is a contest of symmetry, grace, and beauty. In the figure category, women present their sculpted bodies in a one-piece and two-piece posing suit. They perform four quarter-turn poses for a panel of judges while wearing three- to six-inch clear heel platform shoes. Yes, the "pole dancer" kind of clear heels that Chris Rock wants to keep his daughters away from.

By month five, two weeks before the contest, I'm 10 percent body fat, 90 percent muscle; my body is beautiful, starving, and ready to pose in the contest. I have two beautiful posing suits made and purchase a pair of the requisite clear heel shoes. Learning to walk in them proves to be the hardest part. A six-foot-four drag queen offers to teach me to walk with grace. I look 25, have the wisdom of half a century, and can walk like a runway model on the clear heel stilts.

On the day of the contest, I'm dizzy, excited, and starving. My trainer and my sister are backstage to give support – along with friends who are in the audience. I feel a bond with the other women who are competing. Each has her own story of how she got there. I realize I was never in competition with these women, only myself. Finally, it's my turn to pose. I make the quarter-turn poses like a champ in those heels. It takes five minutes. Five minutes after all those months of work! I win second place in the figure category. I lose by one point to a woman 15 years my junior. Afterwards, I overhear people comment "She (meaning me) was robbed." If they only knew! I smile at the compliment and run my hand over the encasement of the Samurai sword I have won and marvel at the engraved title, "2004 NANBF (North America Natural Bodybuilding Federation) Annual Michigan Open, Figure Short Division, Second Place." Robbed? I don't think so. The contest was won five months ago on that bright sunny day when I decided to compete. It was won when I nurtured faith and chose excellence to usher in my 50th year. I had become Queen Midas; confident that anything I touched and invested in would turn to gold.

Most importantly, I learned that faith is a vision of a future that begins with a self firmly rooted in now.

Faith is maintained by keeping the vision of that future alive and always in sight.

Faith is a practice maintained by actions taken, big and small, toward a goal that at times seems impossible and surely unreachable. Faith is compassion; it does not shout or scold my weaknesses. Faith seeks only to strengthen them, that I may reach my intended goal. Faith is impossible to lose, but always vulnerable to be misplaced.

Faith must be practiced and, when practiced, offers the opportunity to get back on track.

If I pick up a pound or two or ten, I don't fear the fat monster anymore. The fat monster has been mastered and swallowed up by my future. From here I can look back, see the bridge that faith and discipline have built, and map the wonders of every step taken.

The future has a fabulous view, darling. No wonder they call it "The Fabulous Fifties!"

Satori Shakoor
Detroit, MI
Age 56
(Picture taken at age 50)

Coach's Commentary

Did these stories spark any ideas? After reading the reinvention stories scattered throughout this book, I hope you see there are no excuses to prevent you from reaching your own reinvention goals.

We must live this life with urgency and purpose. At this age, the one thing that we should ALL know for sure is that tomorrow is not promised. So, what are you waiting for? What excuses are you making for not living your life, NOW?

Fifty, half a century, 50 percent, half full, halfway...

Lots of people are living to 100 years old and beyond, so the idea that it is too late to address the things you want in life is ludicrous, ridiculous, preposterous, and even *nonsensical*. "Heavens to Murgatroyd!" *(Ah...excuse the baby boomer's Saturday cartoon flashback!)*

NOW is exactly the right time to take a leap of faith and pursue your dreams. **Wake up to life.**

Got a pocket full of lemons? Make lemonade. **Rocked by unexpected circumstances?** See opportunity in the waves, instead of crisis on the seas.

Feeling afraid? Acknowledge the fear and then do it anyway!

But, first gird yourself with preparation: **take action**, create the strategy, line up your resources, and follow the undone in your life. Fifty isn't the end – it's the beginning of a quest to get better, stronger, and wiser.

If you've always wanted to go to school – **GO!** If you want to learn how to sky dive – **DO IT!** If you want 6-pack, 3-pack, or just no-flab abs – **GET BUSY!** If you want to write a book, change your look, start a new career or take up a new hobby...take a leap of faith and get started.

Honestly...if not now, WHEN?

Dance as if no one was watching: Dean Moss

Copyright, Marva Goldsmith & Associates, Inc

I didn't know it would take so long or change so much along the way, but looking back there is a certain satisfaction in the journey. Thirty years ago when I was 25, I came to New York City to dance. . The ambition was to be a dance artist and the means was a scholarship invitation from Arthur Mitchell to study at the Dance Theater of Harlem. It was 1979 and I installed myself above some crack retailers on Avenue C in the East Village. That raging illegal enterprise meant the building was "protected" even though the surrounding neighborhood resembled the burnt out remains of war. When I mention this, some wax poetic about "la vie Bohéme," but I just smile. It was the unforeseen beginning of an often painful education; one that would challenge how I thought about myself, my work, and the idea of success.

In dance everyone generally starts their career early and by 40 it's over. When you begin; you may understand that the horizon of change is never far away. Gratefully, the vision of youth is severely limited and mine was particularly so. I wanted to dance and I continually changed my circumstance to enable it. I left DTH after three months, no longer wanting to be only a "ballet boy." I danced modern at the Martha Graham school until she told me herself, kindly, I was too small to be in the company. I then shifted to theater; danced in the first revival of *West Side Story* in Paris. It was fantastic. I came back from abroad thinking I could be a Broadway star and utterly failed. The idea of commercial stardom died a long, excruciating death. I eventually became destitute, forcing me to reconsider my ambitions as an artist. But I had no backup plan so I had to work through it, and I did, successfully auditioning for an acclaimed contemporary dance company that was randomly suggested by a friend.

For the next ten years I danced for David Gordon and the Pick-up Performance Company. We traveled all over the world; from Australia and Japan to Brazil and through Europe. Beginning at $150 a week, it was a long way from the $750 I was making show dancing but I loved it. Success had changed from hi-style and a big theater in Paris to a $135/mo. unheated squat in the South Bronx and working in a deeply creative partnership with a contemporary performance director I admired. Still, time passes and what once was distant was now knocking at the door. As forty loomed I found I needed to make dances instead of just dancing in them. So leaving the nest of a (by then decently) paying company behind, I once again dropped to an embarrassingly low income level as I made ends meet by waiting tables three days a week. I did this for the next six years.

The first review for my own work went like this:

"Dean Moss opens his new trio, dirt with an extended solo for himself, establishing an atmosphere of pure pleasure that is sustained, with interesting variations, throughout the piece. Moss is one of those extravagantly blessed dancers whose every move has beauty in it. He's fluency and grace personified--which might be too much of a good thing if it weren't offset by the strange ability to

embody celestial lightness and rooted weight at the very same time"
-Tobi Tobias for the Village Voice 1992

Great review, yes, but in fact it was "too much of a good thing.". A friend wrote to congratulate me saying, "Ok you win, now what?" What indeed?. I was then making about $800/mo. struggling to pay $500/mo. rent in Brooklyn. In retrospect, the review merely signaled the introduction of a notable artist to the dance community, but it was too much too fast and hard not to be affected by such a grand entry. It took a couple of years for the inevitable fall and when it occurred I had no one to blame save myself. What happened? I traveled to Senegal and described a project that articulated that experience. My audience expected a narrative of some sort and I delivered an abstract and obscure performance. It was badly received. Worse, I felt I had compromised myself by trading on gifts that were perhaps overstated. It made me realize I needed to teach myself about how to make work and also about audience expectation. I needed to develop a new way of seeing much more than myself. I started researching this new practice over the next several years at a community theater in Brooklyn. Which is a fancy way of saying I purposefully hid away for a while and made a lot of bad work while exploring my vision and honing my craft.

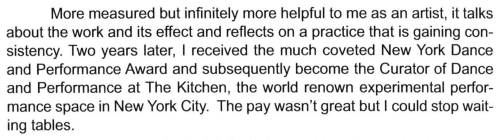

Five years later:

"Moss is a master of theatrical halftones. Everything he concocts contributes to an overall shimmering effect. His worlds have the enticement of whispers; their delicacy makes us pay unusually close attention."
-Robert Greskovic for the Village Voice 1997

More measured but infinitely more helpful to me as an artist, it talks about the work and its effect and reflects on a practice that is gaining consistency. Two years later, I received the much coveted New York Dance and Performance Award and subsequently become the Curator of Dance and Performance at The Kitchen, the world renown experimental performance space in New York City. The pay wasn't great but I could stop waiting tables.

My experience at The Kitchen changed how I perceived my practice. Being a curator, I saw three to four times the performances I saw as an artist and a much broader range of works in a multitude of dance and theater forms. I gained a more nuanced understanding of the New York dance community plus an introduction to the national and international performance scenes. I cultivated a professional image within my community of aesthetic rigor and innovation. In short, it took me out of the isolation of my practice, and gave new perspectives on my place in a global marketplace of artists and art professionals. Ironically, my duties at The Kitchen also included the facilitation of an emerging artist dance composition workshop twice a year.

All of this had a dramatic effect on not only my practice but my life. As I was turning fifty, diligence started to pay off. Small successes and failures began to slowly culminate. The work, mostly known to a small group of dance art insiders, began to be seen locally in venues of higher visibility and internationally. Becoming known for the composition workshop facilitation turned into an invitation to teach for a year in Tokyo. The positive experience in Japan made me think I was capable of high level teaching as a complement to art making. In 2007, a colleague suggested that I apply as a multimedia artist for an Ivy League university position. I thought he was crazy but I did and when the dust settled, I was a Visiting Lecturer in the Department of Visual and Environmental Studies at Harvard University. And, keeping with the theme, in 2011 I will teach in the Theater Studies Department of Yale.

My life has become more effective and less of a struggle. Experience has given me a greater confidence and ambition in what is possible. Looking back, one of the most gratifying developments was the change in my practice as I moved from working in do-it-yourself isolation to initiating several interdisciplinary and multicultural collaborations. I had tended to do everything: choreograph and perform, constructing sets, designing costumes, mixing the audio and producing all the video elements. Over time I learned to render ideas and balance media in ways that create, shape, and sustain tension. But like the otherness of traveling, curation, and the facilitation of artists, I wanted the process of making work to directly challenge and expand my life in the world. In conceiving and constructing collaborative productions, that is exactly what it did.

My most recent project is titled *Nameless Forest*. It is a collaboration with Korean sculptor and installation artist Sungmyung Chun, and also includes imagery and diary entries from a photojournalist plus neon and mirror effects from a visual artist. In all, the production is comprised of a community of fifteen individual collaborators including six amazing performers. It is an exciting work and a wonderful life.

If there's a "take away" perhaps it's this: regardless of how long it takes or when you can start, "do what you love."

Dean Moss
Age 55
New York, NY

Coach's Note:

What can we learn from Dean Moss? For many years, Dean Moss was a talented dancer. But, as his story illustrates, there are a lot of starving dancers whose every movement epitomize talent and grace. Dean established himself as a **leader** in the practice of conceiving multidisciplinary and often trans-cultural collaborative projects. When Dean emerged from the crowded field of talented dancers as an artist working in both dance and video, he captured the imagination of others.

CONCLUSION...

...But Not the End

December 5

There's a party over here!

I hear and feel the familiar thud of the plane doors closing, and the plane shudders into motion. I am on my way to Detroit for my 50th birthday party.

My sister Marcia and my cousins Sheryl, Bernadine, and Preston are hosting friends and family to help me usher in my decade of new beginnings.

We roll toward the runway, and I begin to say a little prayer as we prepare for take-off.

My prayer is one of gratitude. I give thanks for all of the many blessings that God has given me: good health, loving family and friends, the health of my family and friends, a bountiful income, a home, an open heart, an active mind, an enlightened spirit, and all of the blessings that I have yet to receive...

And to that prayer, today I add my gratitude for the role YOU have played in my journey. I am grateful to you for bringing my vision of NOW into a reality.

Peace and blessings,

Marva

APPENDIX

Survey Questions

I conducted a survey of 100 persons over the age of 49. Here's what they said about turning 50 – and living their 6th decade.

Now that you are 50, what do you know for sure?

- Change is a beautiful thing.
- That I don't know anything for sure and the best part is, I don't <u>have</u> to know anything for sure.
- That life is to be celebrated and regrets are a waste of time; learn the lesson and keep moving.
- I know for sure that I still feel the same way inside as I did when I was ten years old, wondering what I will be when I "grow up."
- The happiest people are in careers they enjoy.
- God wants me to love <u>me</u> more and, consequently, love others more, too.
- That life is meant to be enjoyed and the "little stuff" isn't worth destroying relationships over.
- I still love my wife on the good days and like her on bad days.
- No more "buts"…You do not have to know exactly what you want to do, or where you want to go, at all times.
- You can follow a lead and pursue a dream as long as you have the energy to do it.
- There is no one right way to do things and you can be successful figuring out your own way.
- I don't have to be threatened by others who are successful – I can learn from them without feeling like a child. Instead, I'm an equal, with an inquisitive nature, seeking all the wisdom I can gather.
- I need to enjoy life more. Fifty is not an impending doom; it is just another phase of life.
- I'm 65 and I know I'll never go backwards. And I like the scenery from here.

- I still have a lot to offer the world!
- Life just keeps getting better but one can't take it for granted. We must take care of the one body we have.
- A spiritual life, along with family and friends, is essential to finding meaning in life.
- Fifty is not old but as we age, it takes a little more time, money, and effort to stay healthy and youthful.
- I know perhaps even less than I knew (or thought I knew) before. I might be more willing to allow complexity and difficulties to assert themselves, as opposed to trying to simplify and "manage" things.
- Life is too short.
- With age comes wisdom.
- I probably will have to continue working for at least 15 more years.
- Trust but verify. Work before play. Faith is a gift to receive, not a goal to achieve. Learn forever.
- A good part of success is one's mental state (attitude). I'm beyond the halfway mark.
- At 55, I know that I will need to be more health conscious than I have ever been in the past.
- I now know that nothing is more important than family.
- I now know that nothing is worth losing my temper.
- I am 61 and I take a little more care of myself and not so much of others.
- I take vitamins every morning, walk, and I am a little more with God.
- I am settled and grounded. It's a nice feeling.
- I would take to heart the old Southern piece of wisdom: You wouldn't care what people thought of you if you knew how seldom they did.
- Nothing is for certain, or forever.
- Carpe Diem – seize the day!
- Older truly is wiser.
- I am getting old.
- Hot flashes are for real.
- Who my friends are that I can depend on.
- There is still a lot I don't know for sure.
- Sex is better!
- Taking care of my health is important.
- No one is perfect.
- I can do whatever I want to do and be happy!
- I need to get in better physical health.

- If you don't take care of yourself, it will really slow you down.
- "Willingness without action is fantasy." Take action; do not just fantasize.
- Love is always worth the effort. My life is full because of all the loved ones in it.
- I work hard to keep my mind sharp so I can remember every friend I have ever known.
- Life is too short to worry too much (but, of course, I do anyway).
- What other people think of you is unimportant. Be true to yourself.
- I know what I like and what I don't like. And I know what I want to do and what I don't want to do – and I'm not afraid to say "No!"
- I don't like parties. I like to write. I'm a loner who needs people. I know who I am. Exercise makes me feel good. I'm less vain every year.
- Life only gets better, your confidence level rises, and you really don't care what people think – but, I never did.
- I want to do all the things I've put off.
- I did not know anything when I was 30.
- I like me!
- I like to organize people, places, and things.
- I enjoy being with family and friends.
- I no longer need to be a size 10 or 12 for that matter, but I do need to know my blood pressure and cholesterol numbers and be healthy.
- It's not as bad as I expected.
- Things always change.
- Love and affirmation are essential – in any form.
- Loss and pain are inevitable – suffering is optional.
- I know less than I did when I was 20!
- I made a number of mistakes in my career, in my 20s and 30s. However, they have all been great learning experiences.
- I am more confident in my 50s and having more fun.
- I'm a complete person with a great deal of room for continued growth.
- I don't have 50 more years left.
- It sure made all that heartache over turning 40 seem ridiculous.
- I do not know all the answers. In fact, I'm still working on the questions.
- Life really begins at 50.
- I am determined.
- I'm 63. I know that life and time are precious gifts and people, not things, really matter.

- I enjoy life.
- Life is about adjusting to change.
- Being almost 70 is not so bad.
- Life is short. Make the most of every day.
- I speak my mind with confidence. I've earned it.
- Relationships with family and friends are most important in life.
- I know that I'll never know everything I want to know.
- I wouldn't get married before turning 30, at least.
- I'm strong, yet fragile.
- My identity changes to grandmother!
- I still get excited and interested in many things going on around me.
- We all know what makes us happiest. Go there and do not be distracted by the siren songs of pop culture or any other forms of pressure to conform.
- I don't want to be younger, but I wish my body was in better shape.
- The older I get, the less I know. I appreciate my "girl" friends.
- Life is so short, and I have more time behind me than I have in front of me.
- I know that turning 60 is just a finger snap away. I know that the only thing one can count on is change. I know that it is important to live each day to its fullest. I know that it is important to be silly.
- Don't waste time.
- Patience is truly a virtue.
- There is a living God that loves me in spite of me.
- Mirrors are everywhere. When I judge someone, or something, that is my projection. I'm using them or it to project something within me that I either admire or reject.
- I love myself.
- I like me – I'm OK.
- I have more self-confidence and I am more secure.
- I am surer of myself in an uncertain world.
- I have turned the corner.

If you could do one thing over again, what would it be?

- Absolutely nothing! I've loved my journey through good times and bad, so far...
- Abuse my body less.
- Enjoy everything I did more and stay in the moment.
- Nothing.
- Not be afraid to live.
- Watch my health.
- I think everything has gone as it should have. Sometimes I regret getting married right after high school and not going to college – but then I still have had a wonderful life.
- Research careers in my field better. I think I would have eventually worked in academia.
- I would have invested more money earlier.
- Spend more family time with my children when they were younger.
- Take more risks.
- Kiss butt.
- I would have set aside my fears and flown earlier.
- Prepare better financially.
- Get divorced sooner.
- Have more children.
- I would have married a different person than my ex.
- I would have stayed in college and earned a degree.
- Enter therapy earlier.
- Learn a lot more about childhood development before having kids. And appreciate them a lot more while I have them.
- Set educational goals and finish them.
- Pay less attention to the Men in My Life; they are important, but not as paramount as my mother told me they were.
- Keep playing cello.
- Get a master's degree.
- Get into a scientific field.
- Pull my son out of public school by the 2nd grade.
- Make better financial decisions.
- Stay in real estate instead of quitting after the first 6 months, back in 1978.
- I would travel to Europe or to Alaska.
- Finish college.

- Can't think of anything that wouldn't have a ripple effect on things I wouldn't want to change. So I've accepted my faults and mistakes, tried to learn from them, and I'm looking ahead.
- Not marry.
- Stay in school and get an advanced degree before having a family, and travel the world.
- Enjoy my teenage years.
- Say "No" more often and not be such a people pleaser.
- Date more before marriage.
- Be a stricter parent.
- I would have embraced my twenties and early thirties instead of wishing I was older.
- I would have worn my bathing suit proudly instead of always covering up!!
- I would have been more aggressive (in a good way) in trying to make all my good ideas come to life. I backed off too much.
- I would have danced more.
- I would go to art school.
- My career choice – I would go directly into filmmaking instead of doing it in mid-career.
- I don't live with regrets – not worth the while!
- Not bail out of my marriage so fast; should have given it a better chance to survive.
- Nothing, I'm "just fine" – can't go back, only forward.
- Marry better & later in life (Married at 17, had kids at 19).
- I suppose I would have gotten rid of my ex earlier and I would have taken more history in college and fewer courses from the lefty radicals – fun though they were.
- Pay attention in college! Meet and befriend those who do not look like me.
- Have sex a lot earlier and with a lot more men!
- Talk more frankly with my mother; she died almost a year ago.
- Spend time with Kevin in the cottage.
- Fulfill my aspirations to be an entrepreneur at an earlier age.
- I wish I had known myself better at an earlier age – like 21.
- Spend more quality, non-hassled time with my daughter.
- Enter marriage with more long-term thought and less emotion.
- Keep contact with everyone I have met in a much better way.

- Change jobs 15 years ago...or go in a different direction right out of college.
- Go to law school.
- Marry my 2nd husband first.
- I would have worked harder to have understood one of my sons when he was a teenager.
- Know more about the law and medicine.
- Be an artist.
- I would not have married at 19.
- I would have asked my ex-husband to leave several years before I finally did and created a much more fulfilling and less-stressed life for all of us sooner than I did.
- I'd redo the educational experience, beginning with college and continue toward a Ph.D.
- Realize how quickly your family grows up and stay more in the present.
- I was raising my children in the late Sixties and Seventies, the height of the feminist movement and its attendant insanities. I was stupid enough to respond by trying to prove my worth – a housewife had no worth in that world. It is not to say that the movement did not improve life for women, but back then feminism was strident and did not recognize what its mission should have included – a choice to not burn your bra.
- Not so much partying in my 20s.
- I wouldn't dress my four girls alike.
- Love more men and stay single.
- I would have started my candy business sooner.
- Marry my first love.
- Be a more understanding husband.

What has been the most exciting change that you have experienced during this last half-century?

- The change in consciousness in America that we just witnessed in the 2008 presidential campaign.
- Accepting myself.
- Realizing I care about myself more than I care about what people think of me.
- I've become what I always wanted to be.
- Finding that there is still time to make a positive difference in the world.
- Civil Rights Movement
- Realizing that I am in control and only I have power over my feelings.
- The knowledge of the world extending beyond home – other climates, cultures and geography.
- I now live alone. Finally, I am all right with it. As a matter of fact, it's exciting to see what options are here for me at this age.
- Buying my company and watching it and my employees grow. And my second marriage to my true soul mate.
- Magellan, Garmin and GPS; Google Earth!
- A tremendous sense of freedom! I have always known myself to be a "late bloomer," and the time has come to bloom. I feel a deep confidence in my instincts and a willingness to hear correction that makes sense. I'm not afraid to try and not afraid to fail.
- Enjoying hobbies and personal interests more.
- More women in politics! And I keep trying to work to get more women elected so I get our half in my lifetime.
- Owning my own business.
- Traveling the world, seeing my children become successful in their own right, getting to know my granddaughters and spending time with them, seeing my mom grow old in good health and good spirits, sharing great times with friends and family, having a wonderful federal career and then a successful business, and creating wealth – all wonderful.
- Being an aunt, great aunt and grandparent. Children bring smiles, hugs, kisses, and squeals of love and affection that just make my heart sing.
- Personally, my personal growth. Globally, the Internet.

- The Internet – by far a life-altering method of communication that has opened up my horizons beyond my little world.
- Becoming a grandmother and great-grandmother.
- The freedom to live in the center of activity via the Internet.
- Virtual communication.
- The end of the Cold War and its existential threat.
- Space exploration.
- Being able to travel to places that I have never visited before (especially via cruises).
- I've fallen in love and gotten married; I've returned to the real estate field.
- The most exciting change in my life has been to move to the USA, a new culture. To live in a society with rights and in a democracy.
- The transition into the computer and communication age.
- Opportunities for women are growing – not as quickly as we 60s feminists hoped – but enough to give us continued hope for our daughters and granddaughters.
- Liberation.
- Gaining extensive knowledge about so many different things (personal and professional) and earning financial freedom.
- I am happily married.
- Not only knowing that I have freedoms, such as financial and emotional, but going with it.
- Understanding God's love and loving who I am.
- Starting a more active lifestyle.
- Education and travel.
- Growing in my spirituality.
- Global awareness, computers.
- Respect for women and people of other races and cultures has increased greatly.
- Medical technology.
- Going from smart paper processing to very smart electronics.
- I'm thrilled to be living now and seeing this presidential election. When I was born, it would not have been imagined.
- Becoming myself.
- Enjoying life to the fullest.
- Wisdom and patience.
- Approaching greater racial, gender and religious equity.
- Growth and respect of women in all fields.

- I birthed two daughters. I birthed myself out of a bad marriage. I know I can birth myself again if I want. I have grandchildren who know and accept me more and more. I wrote a book and started an association. I maintain a great professional reputation; am a dutiful, beloved daughter, and part of a positive, loving relationship.
- Advent of the Internet.
- Owning my own business and becoming self-directed.
- Divorce!
- Falling in true, true love.
- Becoming a mother.
- Getting married.
- Communication advances...Internet...cell phones.
- I have loved watching my daughter grow up and now about to be married.
- Personally, maturing and liking myself more. Change in the world, the ease and speed of communication.
- Use of the computer.
- Better hair color.
- Being a grandmother.
- Technology...and I don't necessarily think it's been a wholly positive change.
- Giving birth and continuing to watch my children blossom. Carving new pathways in science that are making a difference.
- Obviously, technological advances, but I don't necessarily see all of them as positive. I HATE walking in the streets, riding the subways, etc., seeing everyone with their ears plugged up, missing the sounds of city, nature, not paying any attention to what's going on around them.
- Everyone is so self-absorbed, especially the youth.
- To see my kids grow up; to begin a new career; to feel strong, healthy, happy.
- Progress in medicine – I'm old enough to remember clearly what could kill you in the 50s and 60s. SO much progress in treatments and cures.
- Personally, raising children. Worldwide...the technology EXPLOSION.
- At 45, after my youngest left for college, I opened my own childcare center. This September, we celebrate our 25th anniversary – you can have it all, just not in the same year.

- Giving birth to my son, finishing a Ph.D., getting a contract for my first book, and rekindling my love for a former lover.
- Well, I think I have finally grown up. What a concept!
- The development of the African-American middle class.
- I finally learned to have a balanced life between work, family and fun. I'm having more fun than at any age of my life. I am dancing – really!
- My self-assuredness; my love of experiencing the moment, and being adventuresome.

The Authors

MARVA L. GOLDSMITH, a Certified Image Professional, helps clients create a road map and understand the role that image and personal branding – the packaging of talents and signature traits into a marketable image – play in their journey.

Marva knows the transformation process intimately because she has lived it. She began her career as an electrical engineer and later became a federal lobbyist and human resources strategist. Now, she uses her experience and diverse skill set to assist her clients with their professional transformation.

Marva studied image management with Dominique Isbecque International, the London Image Institute, and the Image Resource Group. She has a Bachelor of Science from Michigan State University in Electrical Engineering and a Master's of Public Administration from Harvard University. She received additional leadership training through the Center for Creative Leadership and Georgetown University's Leadership Coaching Program. She is a certified Reach Brand Strategist.

CARLA DANCY SMITH is a "change coach." She partners with individuals and offers tools and techniques to help them change directions during milestone events. She offers workshops to teens advancing from middle school to high school and to students graduating from high school and progressing to college. She coaches individuals making a transition from one employment to a new endeavor, or retirement.

Carla teaches diversity courses as an adjunct instructor and is a qualified Myers-Briggs Type Indicator (MBTI) assessment administrator. She has a Master's of Science in Organization Development (MSOD) from the American University/National Training Laboratory (AU/NTL) located in Washington, D.C.; and a Bachelor of Science in Business Administration from Rockhurst Jesuit College in Kansas City, Missouri. Carla has written and published articles, given speeches, is a member of many professional organizations, and prides herself on being a life-long learner.

ART LIZZA is a freelance writer with over 30 years' experience in scholarly publishing. Art resides in the relative wilderness of northwest New Jersey. He is adept at all facets of writing, from conception, editing, and copy editing to digital composition/manufacturing, printing, CD & DVD production, and electronic delivery of publishing content. Art's motto: "Uncompromising dedication to excellence, clarity, and accuracy."

SUE THOMPSON is the principal of Set Free Life Seminars, a speaking and training resource offering insights to help people become what they were meant to be: contributing confidently to life. She has a Master's in Clinical Psychology. Sue is a personality expert and etiquette trainer, and speaks to companies and organizations throughout the country.

SATORI SHAKOOR is a published writer, produced playwright, and a veteran of live performance. Satori received a 2007 NAACP Theatre Award for "Best Ensemble Cast" for her role as Ms. Enid in *Da Kink in My Hair*. She has recorded and toured as one of The Brides of Funkenstein and with George Clinton's Parliament Funkadelic. Satori has worked with multiple Grammy award winners including David Foster, the late Sly Stone, and the late Luther Vandross. She was an opening act for Joan Rivers, has appeared at The Improv, The Comedy Store, and Yuk Yuk's. Theatre and film credits: *Harlem Duet, Boy Gets Girl, The Adventures of a Black Girl in Search of God, Menopause: The Musical!* and *The Hurricane*. Satori has written sketch comedy for Canadian television and her short story, "How I Took a Menopause" is published in an anthology entitled, *Midlife Clarity: Epiphanies of Grown Up Girls*. For more info, visit: www.myspace.com/satorishakoor.

ALICIA M. NAILS is an Emmy-award winning television producer and journalist with more than twenty years' experience documenting and communicating the African-American experience in both local and national media. She currently directs the Journalism Institute for Minorities at Wayne State University in Detroit, Michigan. Alicia has written and produced at WTVS (PBS) and WJBK (Fox 2) in Detroit, WXIA (Atlanta), and for the formerly nationally syndicated *Essence* television program. She is currently a writer/editor at WWJ News Radio 950 in Detroit. Previously the National Marketing Director for United Methodist Communications in New York City, Alicia has extensive event organization skills, including special event production for the United Negro College Fund's Atlanta and Detroit offices where she coordinated community and corporate leaders in fundraising events: the UNCF Parade of Stars Telethon, The Mayors' Scholarship Ball, and the *Ebony* Fashion Fair. An attorney, Alicia is licensed to practice in Michigan and Illinois.

RICHARD DEAN MOSS followed his love of dance to New York City where he lives with his wife Kay Takeda. Dean is a director, choreographer and media artist. He has performed all over the world in countries that include Japan, Korea, China, Great Britain, France, Italy, Brazil, South Africa, and Indonesia. For five years Dean was the Curator of Dance and Performance at the internationally renowned experimental performance space, The Kitchen, NYC. He taught for a year as Guest Professor at the Tokyo National University of Fine Arts and Music and for two years as a Visiting Lecturer in the Department of Visual and Environmental Studies at Harvard University which was acknowledged with a Certificate of Distinction in Teaching from the Derek Bok Center for Teaching and Learning. Dean will have artistic residencies at both Arizona and Florida state universities in the fall of 2010. In the spring semester of 2011, he will begin his appointment as Artist Lecturer in the department of Theater Studies at Yale University.

Made in the USA
Lexington, KY
26 March 2011